£1.00

Pet Owner's Guide to
THE
GOLDEN RETRIEVER

Bernard Bargh

RINGPRESS

RINGPRESS

Published by Ringpress Books Limited,
PO Box 8, Lydney, Gloucestershire
GL15 6YD, United Kingdom.

First Published 1993
Reprint 1996
© 1993 Ringpress Books Limited.
All rights reserved

ISBN 0 948955 43 0

Printed in Hong Kong through Printworks Int. Ltd.

Contents

About the author

Bernard Bargh has been involved with Golden Retrievers all his life, breeding, exhibiting and judging the breed. He has enjoyed considerable success in the show ring, and his Carasan kennels are well-known for producing top-quality puppies. In 1990 he owned the top Golden Retriever in the UK, Ch. Moonsprite Mermaid of Carasan, who, the following year took the coveted award of Best of Breed at Crufts.

Bernard is an international Championship show judge, and has been Chairman of the North West Golden Retriever Club for eleven years. He is a regular contributor to the English weekly dog paper, *Dog World*.

Acknowledgements

My thanks to Mavis Chapman who has typed the manuscript, Valerie Foss for all her help and advice, and Patrick Stapleton, Deputy General Manager of the Pembroke Hotel, Blackpool, where most of this book was written.

Thanks also to Pat Tuck, Sheila Watkins, Dave and Sue Barnes, and Roger Harvey Garden World, Stevenage, Herts, for co-operation with photographs. We are most grateful to David Dalton and *Dog World* for permission to use the grooming and trimming photographs, and also to the Guide Dogs for the Blind Association for their help and co-operation.

Bernard Bargh pictured with Ch. Moonsprite Mermaid of Carasan.

Chapter One

IN THE BEGINNING

A BRIEF HISTORY

The Golden Retriever, as a breed, was evolved by Dudley Coutts Marjoribanks, first Lord Tweedmouth (1820-1894), on his estate, Guisachan, in Scotland. The name 'Golden Retriever' came later; they were firstly known as Yellow Retrievers. It was believed that Lord Tweedmouth had seen a troupe of Russian circus dogs performing, and was so taken by their intelligence that he had bought the whole troupe. He then, reputedly, took the dogs to Scotland to use on his estate, and bred them among themselves.

This romantic theory was disproved by a famous breeder and breed historian, Mrs Elma Stonex. With the help of the sixth Earl of Ilchester, a relative of the first Lord Tweedmouth, they proved the dogs were of Scottish origin. Among information used to substantiate this claim was the Stud Book, kept by the first Lord Tweedmouth, which can be seen today at the Kennel Club in London, England.

This recorded that Lord Tweedmouth's first Yellow Retriever was a single yellow pup from a litter of black wavy-coated pups. The yellow pup was obtained from a Brighton cobbler, who had got the puppy from a gamekeeper. This puppy, called Nous, was born in June 1864, and was the foundation sire of the breed.

In his kennels, Lord Tweedmouth had some Tweed Water Spaniels; a breed which is now extinct. However, early writings describe these dogs as small, ordinary English Retrievers of a liver colour. In those days the term 'liver' covered all the sandy colours. One of the Tweed Water Spaniels called Belle was mated to Nous, and she produced four puppies. Of these, one dog, Crocus was given to his eldest son; two bitches, Cowslip and Primrose, were kept, and the other bitch, Ada, was given to Lord Tweedmouth's nephew, the fifth Earl of Ilchester, who began the Ilchester line.

Lord Tweedmouth found that a black dog mated to a yellow bitch invariably produced yellow puppies, and from the Stud Book we see how he planned his litters and evolved his strain of working retrievers from 1868 to 1890. Cowslip was mated to Tweed (a Tweed Water Spaniel), and their daughter, Topsy, was mated to a black wavy-coated Retriever and produced Zoe. She, in turn, was mated to Jack, who was the result of a mating between Cowslip and Sampson, an Irish Setter.

The last two Yellow Retrievers recorded in Lord Tweedmouth's Stud Book were Prim and Rose, born in 1889 and they show what a skilful breeder Lord Tweedmouth was. Puppies were given to friends and relations, and they were first exhibited at a dog show in England in 1908 by Lord Harcourt, of the Culham kennels – and all his dogs went back to Lord Tweedmouth's breeding.

Mr McDonald, who was head keeper to the Earl of Shrewsbury, was important in the early foundation of the breed with his Ingestre kennels, and at about the same time Mrs W. Charlesworth started her Noranby kennels, which were the most influential in the breed for the next forty years, until her death in 1951. In 1913 Golden Retrievers were given a separate register at the Kennel Club in London under the name Retrievers (Golden, Yellow). In America the breed was first recognised by the American Kennel Club in 1932.

CHOOSING A GOLDEN RETRIEVER
Owning a dog will drastically alter your life for some ten years, or more, and so the first decision you have to make is whether you should own a dog in the first place. Remember, care and attention is necessary 365 days a year – including Christmas Day – the dog doesn't know it's a festive holiday!

The next important matter to consider is your choice of dog. You may well admire the beautiful appearance of a Golden Retriever, but is the breed suited to your lifestyle? Such matters as size, coat, and breed characteristics must all be weighed up. The questions you must ask yourself at the outset are:
1. Does the house that I live in lend itself to a relatively large dog?
2. Will the dog be left alone in the house for long periods, while I am out at work?
3. Am I active and fit enough to give a Golden the correct amount of exercise?
4. Do I have the time and patience to spend grooming a long-coated breed?
5. Can I afford to buy the necessary food to feed a large dog?

BREED CHARACTERISTICS
There is a song with the lines: "Beautiful to look at, delightful to behold," and so is a Golden Retriever, with its glamorous long, golden coat, which requires constant attention and grooming, and, as a result, the breed may not be entirely suitable for the house-proud.

The behaviour patterns of your dog as a domestic pet will be strongly influenced by the work it was originally bred to do. The Golden Retriever was bred from the beginning to do a job of work in the field as a gundog, retrieving shot or wounded game to its handler, hence its obsession with carrying things. Your Golden will always be wanting to bring 'presents' to you, and in order to avoid mishaps, it is advisable to make sure your dog has plenty of toys of its own to carry around the house. In the process of bringing you a present, your Golden will never stop wagging its tail – so watch out for those valuable ornaments on low-lying tables. No use 'playing hell' after HE has inadvertently smashed your most prized possession!

Being a working dog, it is imperative that your Golden gets a considerable amount of exercise, then it will be quite happy to curl up in its own quiet corner of the house, enjoying the company of its 'devoted' owner.

TEMPERAMENT
Although a comparatively large breed, most Goldens possess a gorgeous, gentle temperament, and show infinite patience with boisterous young children, coupled with a gentleness with young babies and old people. They are blessed with extreme intelligence which is developed by human contact, hence the necessity for a single pet Golden to live in the house, where it will always be anxious to please, and will warn of any intruders.

The Golden possesses a superb temperament – gentle with children, loyal to its owners, and it is also highly intelligent and eager to please.

The Golden Retriever is a gundog, bred for its ability to retrieve game.

It is hard to resist a beautiful puppy, but the Golden Retriever grows into a sizeable long-coated dog that will require regular grooming, exercise, and a well-balanced diet.

Golden Retrievers love cars, and they cannot wait to leap in the back of a car, ever hopeful of an outing.

A dog, of course, cannot speak a language, but before long, your Golden, living in the house, will understand every word you utter and will be able to tell you the time – especially when meal times are at hand. Goldens love cars and the very noise of keys being jangled will be a cause of great excitement; a sure sign that an outing is imminent. My old dog Sandy (Janville Laurel of Carasan) once went missing for a whole morning, and despite numerous search parties we couldn't find him anywhere. Eventually, I went to the garage and, yes, you've guessed it, there was Sandy fast asleep on the back seat of the car, completely oblivious to all the panic going on around him!

If you decide that a Golden Retriever is the right breed for you, then you will have opened up a new dimension in your life. With luck, your Golden will live to around twelve years of age, but will remain a puppy all its life, thriving on love and attention coupled with discipline. In return, you will be repaid a thousand times by trust, affection and companionship.

Chapter Two

BUYING A PUPPY

If you have decided that the Golden Retriever is the breed for you, it is very important that all the family should be in complete agreement about taking on the responsibilities of owning a dog. They must all realise that the tasks – and some of them are just that – will have to be shared by everyone. Obviously the person who is most at home during the day will do the bulk of the caring, and it is better if one person is responsible for the feeding. A feeding routine, especially in puppyhood, is of great importance, and this should not be trusted to a child who is liable to forget exactly when a meal is due, or even worse, to forget to feed the puppy at all!

FINDING A PUPPY
When you are ready to go out and buy your puppy, the golden rule is to buy from a breeder of Golden Retrievers, and not from kennels who advertise every breed under the sun. A specialised breeder will have fed and looked after the mother (dam) correctly, and you will probably be able to see her, and possibly the grandmother, and other close relations, when you call to see the pups. You can be confident that the pups will have been reared to the best of the breeder's ability, and you can be sure that the litter has received the right sort of food, with the required vitamins. A breed specialist will also pay attention to the question of hereditary defects such as hip dysplasia and cataracts (see Chapter 8: Health Care). The puppies will have been regularly groomed; they will have had the correct amount of exercise for their age, and you will be charged a fair and reasonable price.

FINDING A BREEDER
How do you find a reputable breeder? All countries have a national Kennel Club, and they keep a list of breed clubs. Find a Golden Retriever Club in your area, contact the secretary, and he/she will put you in touch with a breeder. The secretary will probably know of someone who actually has a litter of pups due. You could also buy the specialised dog papers (available both weekly and monthly), where breeders are listed.
    Another option is to contact your local vet to see if one of his clients has any Golden puppies, or perhaps you have seen someone in the street with a lovely puppy, and they will only be too pleased to tell you which breeder they bought it from.
    When you visit the breeder, do not be surprised if you are cross-questioned as to your suitability to own one of their carefully reared puppies. Most responsible breeders want to make sure that their puppies are going to good homes where they

Taking on a puppy is a big responsibility, and the whole family must be prepared to take on the commitment.

It is helpful if you can see the parents when you go to choose a puppy.

If you choose a female and you are keeping her purely as a companion, it is advisable to have her neutered.

In Goldens, the males are just as loving as the females, but they are bigger and heavier.

will be properly looked after. You will be asked where is the puppy going to be housed? Is your garden well-fenced? How long will the puppy be left on its own? How many children do you have, and what are their ages? If the breeder is satisfied that you can provide the right sort of home for a Golden Retriever, you will be asked to pay a small deposit in order to reserve a puppy. The balance will be due when you eventually collect your puppy.

MALE OR FEMALE?

One of the most important decisions to be made at this stage is whether you wish to have a male (dog) or female (bitch). In Goldens, the dogs are just as loving as the bitches, but they are bigger and heavier. Bitches, of course, come in season twice a year; they always cast their coat and get a new one before actually starting their season. Looking after an in-season bitch can be extremely difficult. The whole family needs to be on guard for the twenty-one days the bitch is on heat; given half a chance, she will be out looking for a mate of her choice, which could result in an unwanted litter nine weeks later.

It is often said that all bitches need one litter; this is an old wives' tale with no foundation in fact. If you do decide to have a bitch, and you are keeping her purely as a companion, you would be well advised to consult your vet as to the best time to have her neutered (spayed). Following the operation, which is usually performed after the bitch has had one season, you will encounter no further problems, with the possible exception of ensuring that the bitch does not put on too much weight.

SELECTING A PUPPY

Having made the decision concerning a dog or a bitch, you are now ready to arrange a time to go and see the puppies. The breeder will probably want you to call before feeding time, as puppies soon fall asleep after they have been fed. By this time, the puppies will be about five weeks old and, to you, they will all look the same. How do you pick one out, and what should you be looking for? Naturally you will have to be guided by the breeder, but there are certain points which you should look for.

The puppies should be lively, alert and friendly. Do not fall for the pup hiding away in a corner; shyness at this stage could indicate an uncertain temperament. The puppies should be sturdy and nicely plump. Distended stomachs indicate worm infestation, and in a carefully reared litter the worming programme should have been underway for some three weeks. When you look at an individual puppy it should smell nice, and when you stroke it there should be no evidence of scabs under the coat on the skin, nor should there be any discharge from the ears or the eyes.

The teeth (the ones you will see are the first teeth, which will be replaced by the second teeth at about four to five months) should be in the form of a scissor bite, i.e. the top teeth overlapping the bottom teeth. At this stage the eye colour will be grey, which gradually changes to a permanent dark brown, and the nose will be jet black, although later in life some of this pigmentation is often lost.

Most puppy buyers have strong views on the question of colour. In most Golden Retriever litters, the colours usually vary between shades of cream and gold, and whenever possible I like to let the customer have a puppy in the colour of their choice. It is important to bear in mind that the eventual colour of your Golden will be the colour of its ears, when a puppy. Puppies are ready to go to their new homes at seven to eight weeks. Never buy a puppy from someone who says it can go earlier – you will be buying trouble. It is not natural for a puppy to be taken away from its littermates at an earlier age. If you have picked your puppy at five weeks, the breeder will probably mark it with some safe vegetable dye or snip the curl from the end of its tail, so you will know which is yours when you go to pick it up. The breeder will probably ask you to call for your puppy in the morning, so that your new pride and joy will have all day to settle into strange surroundings. Meanwhile, you now have about two weeks to make preparations for your new arrival.

Before your puppy arrives home, there are certain preparations which should be made, so that your pup gets off to a good start.

HOUSING AND BEDDING
The first thing to decide is where your puppy is going to live, and what sort of bed is required. Golden Retrievers are a very loving breed, and they should be treated as such – one dog on its own must *always* live in the house, *never* in an outside kennel.

In most cases, the kitchen is deemed to be the most suitable place for your puppy to sleep, and the next question is what sort of bed is required? It may be wise to start off with a cardboard box, lined with a blanket, first ensuring that any sharp metal staples have been removed. You can then graduate to a more permanent bed, and there are many different types on the market. The plastic, kidney-shaped beds have the advantage of being easy to clean, and they are sufficiently hard and strong, so that puppies do not find them particularly chewable.

Remember to buy a bed that is big enough for an adult Golden Retriever, and this will need to be a minimum of thirty-six inches in diameter. In addition, you will require two blankets or pads to fit in the plastic bed. Ideal for the purpose is an absorbent fleece, which is machine-washable and can be dried very quickly. The reason for having two pieces is so that you always have a spare when you need to wash the bedding. Canine duvets or pet bean-bags also make suitable bedding; always make sure you buy an extra cover for both types.

EQUIPMENT YOU REQUIRE
FEEDING BOWLS
You will require two dog bowls, one for food and one for water. It is worth buying a stainless steel bowl for the food bowl, as this type is easy to clean and will last for years. A ceramic china bowl is best for the water, as, due to its weight it cannot be easily tipped over.

COLLAR AND LEAD
It is a good idea to fit a small, lightweight collar at a very early age. You will find that your puppy will scratch at the collar for a while, but most will soon get used to the strange sensation. I usually leave the collar on for approximately two hours, then I remove it, and repeat the procedure later in the day.

Once the puppy has accepted the collar, I, personally do not keep one on all the time. I find it creates a ridge around the hair, which is detrimental to showing. However, what is far more important for the well-being of the dog is to ensure that you increase the size of the collar as the puppy grows. A dog must *never* be fitted

There is a big range of feeding bowls on the market, but I would recommend a stainless steel food bowl, and a ceramic china bowl for water.

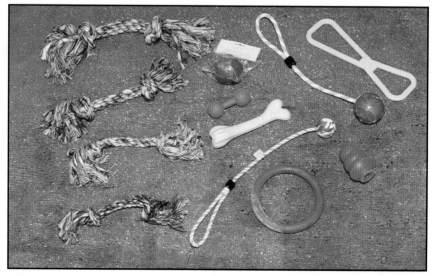

The best toys to buy for your puppy are tough, cotton raggers, which are virtually indestructable. Beware of rubber toys as a puppy can chew bits off.

Get your puppy off to the right start and you will be rewarded with a wonderful companion.

with a collar that is too small. At this stage, a lightweight lead can be attached to the collar. To begin with, allow the puppy to run free, with the lead attached, and eventually you can graduate to holding the lead.

GROOMING EQUIPMENT
You will also need to buy a brush and comb, even though your puppy will require a minimum of grooming attention in the first few months. However, it is important that your puppy gets used to standing still while you give a quick brush, using a bristle brush. I use a 'half-comb', which is made of steel and measures 7in in length. There are 24 teeth on one side and 37 on the other, and I find this ideal for teasing out the odd knot or tangle in the featherings. All puppies can get a bit sticky after eating, and you should try to sponge off the worst of this after meals.

TOYS
It is worth buying a few toys which can be carried by your puppy, and will also help with the chewing. A word of caution: do not buy anything so small that it could get caught in your puppy's throat, and do not buy any toys made of rubber, which could result in small pieces being chewed off.
On the subject of items being carried, remember you are buying a Golden Retriever, and that means your dog will constantly want to carry presents to you. If one of these 'treasures' happens to be something you do not want the dog to have, such as a slipper or a shoe, gently take it from your puppy's mouth, and replace it with one of the toys that is allowed. The idea of this is to teach the puppy to bring things to you; if you always take the item away without replacing it, you will soon get a puppy that runs off in the opposite direction.

PLAY-PEN
One other item of equipment which comes in very useful, is a puppy play-pen. It can be used to confine the puppy in the kitchen on the occasions when you have to go out, and you do not wish to give the pup the run of the entire room. Most play-pens are made of wire-mesh, ideally it should measure 36ins x 25ins x 27ins, and it has the advantage of being easy to fold away and store when it is not in use.

ARRIVING HOME
At last, the great day arrives when it is time to collect your puppy – and one thing is certain, your life will never be the same again. For the next six months your puppy will need attention morning, noon, and hopefully, not too much at night.
I have always found the best way to collect a puppy is for someone else to drive the car, and to hold the puppy on my lap, which is covered with a thick towel. Make sure you have some newspapers and paper towels within easy reach, in case of accidents. Some puppies are never car-sick; they just curl up on your lap and go to sleep, but it is a good idea to be prepared! Most sensible breeders do not feed a puppy before the journey, so minimising the chance of such accidents. If you have to travel alone, the puppy play-pen can be put to good use.

THE PAPERWORK
When you collect your puppy, the breeder should give you a folder containing some important documents, plus some useful information sheets. It should include:

KENNEL CLUB REGISTRATION CERTIFICATE: This proves that the dog is pure-bred, and there is a section for you to fill in and send off to the Kennel Club so that the puppy can be transferred into your ownership. Established breeders use kennel names, which are called prefixes. My prefix is Carasan, and all the dogs I breed carry this name, followed by another of my choice, e.g. Carasan Colonel, Carasan Clementine, Carasan Henrietta etc. If I buy a puppy from another kennel, then I add my prefix to the end of the name. For instance, I bought a puppy from the Moonsprite kennels, and was lucky enough to make her into a Champion. Her full title is Ch. Moonsprite Mermaid of Carasan.

PEDIGREE: The breeder should provide you with a copy of your puppy's pedigree. Most pedigree forms allow the space for five generations. The top half concerns the breeding of the sire (father), and the bottom half relates to the dam (mother). All Champions are either written in, or underlined in red.

DIET SHEET: It is advisable to keep to the diet the breeder has been feeding for the first few days at least. Your puppy will have more than enough to cope with settling into a new home and a new family, without the added trauma of a change of diet. Some breeders will supply you with enough food for the first 24 hours or longer.

INSURANCE COVER: This is rarely provided in the USA, but in the UK many reputable breeders provide new owners with insurance which covers the puppy for a period of six weeks from the date of sale. At the end of this period, the insurance company make contact to see if the new owner wants to continue the policy. Bearing in mind the cost of a puppy, plus veterinary fees, this may be a wise investment.

THE FIRST NIGHT
This can be a traumatic time for both puppy and owner. The puppy will feel very lost, spending the first night away from the warmth and comfort of littermates, and you should do your best to make it settle easily. Many people have their own ideas on the best way of doing this, but I think that warmth is an essential ingredient. If your puppy has been fed, and you make sure the bed is warm, possibly providing a toy for the pup to snuggle up to, hopefully, sleep will win the day!

THE FIRST WEEKS
HOUSE TRAINING
This, if done properly, will take more of your time during the first few weeks than any other task. The secret is that the moment your puppy wakes up, or finishes a meal, you take it outside *immediately*, and give lots of praise when your pup does the necessary. It is no use putting the pup out alone; you must go out too, come hail, rain or snow! Do not chastise your pup for the odd 'mistake' in the house, at this stage. At this very young age, a pup has no real control over the bodily functions, and it is really your fault for not anticipating your pup's needs.

At night, place a newspaper on the floor by the door, and you will be amazed how quickly your puppy gets the message. Don't forget to praise your pup in the morning if the newspaper has been used. One final tip, make an effort to get up earlier than usual, and you might even beat your pup to it!

When choosing a puppy, it is interesting to watch the littermates play together, and you can learn something of their personalities.

The puppies should look sturdy and nicely plump; they should be lively, alert and friendly.

Your puppy has to get used to lots of new experiences, and it must learn to get on with all the members of its new family.

If you decide to use a complete diet, fresh water must be available at all times.

FINDING A VET

Like a good doctor, a good vet is worth his or her weight in gold, and it is worth talking to 'doggy' friends in your neighbourhood, who will probably recommend a practice. In most cases, your puppy's first visit to the vet will be for the essential inoculations which provide protection against Leptospirosis, Hepatitis, Distemper, and Parvovirus.

When your puppy arrives home at seven to eight weeks of age, it may not have received any inoculations, and will therefore be very vulnerable. You should not take your puppy outside your own house and garden until two weeks after the final injection, and you should not allow the pup to come into contact with other dogs during that time. Different vets use different products, and this affects the start the inoculation programme, and the interval between injections. My vet inoculates at eight or ten weeks, followed by a second injection at twelve weeks. This means that the earliest the puppy can go out into the big, wide world is fourteen weeks. It is wise to start socialisation as soon as possible after this period of isolation, so that your puppy gets used to all sorts of different experiences as soon as possible. This will aid your dog's mental development, and will prevent problems in later life.

WORMING

Your puppy should have been wormed three times by the time you take charge. Puppies invariably have roundworms, and so it is advisable to worm every two weeks until your puppy is twelve weeks old, then once a month until your pup is twelve months old, and two or three times a year thereafter. On one of these occasions, use a dual-purpose wormer, which covers tapeworm as well as roundworm. Your vet will recommend a suitable brand, and advise you on dosage.

EXERCISE

For the first four months, do not fall into the temptation of over-exercising a young puppy. The muscles are not developed, and too much exercise can hamper development. The puppy will get all the exercise that is needed by running free around the garden, plus *very* short walks when the socialisation period begins.

SLEEP

A puppy requires plenty of peaceful, uninterrupted sleep, as much as a human baby, in fact. It is vital to remember that a puppy is not a plaything, and children must not be allowed to disturb the puppy when it wants to sleep. A tired puppy soon becomes irritable, and you could be creating future problems if you do not allow your puppy to have adequate rest periods.

FEEDING

A healthy, balanced diet is essential for the well-being of your Golden Retriever, but nowadays there are so many different types of dog food and methods of feeding, that it can be quite baffling for the new owner trying to decide on the best diet to offer. There are basically four different methods of feeding your dog:

COMPLETE FEEDS

These usually come in some pellet form, and as the name implies, they are 'complete', containing everything your dog needs. They are nutritionally balanced, and include all the vitamins and other additives that your dog requires. In most cases, there are different complete diets available to meet particular requirements, such as puppy growth, general adult maintenance, dogs in working conditions, and nursing bitches. The diet can be fed dry, or soaked. However, if it is fed dry it is essential to make sure that plenty of fresh water is available at all times.

ORTHODOX
Canned meat or unrefined tripe, plus soaked biscuits, with various additives. The quality of canned dog food does vary, and the owner would be well advised to examine the breakdown of contents closely (listed on the label), before deciding on which brand to feed.

NATURAL
Meat, fed raw. Nowadays the pet owner has to rely on getting 'human consumption' meat from butchers or supermarket. With this method, meat and biscuits are not fed together. The biscuit is always wholemeal, and vegetables and herbs complete the diet.

VEGETARIAN
Although the dog is a carnivore, vegetarian dog owners may not wish to have meat in the house. There are now specially manufactured vegetarian diets, which come as a complete feed, and these will provide your dog with a balanced diet.

Every dog owner finds the method of feeding that is the most convenient for their particular lifestyle, and the type of food that suits the individual dog. However, there are a some useful tips, which are worth bearing in mind:
1. Dogs are creatures of habit, and regular mealtimes are a must.
2. Never leave food down indefinitely; if it is not eaten within ten minutes, then it should be thrown away.
3. Always serve food at room temperature, never straight from the refrigerator.
   I have always fed what I call the 'Orthodox Method' – meat, plus soaked biscuit, and listed below is the diet sheet I give to new owners when collecting their puppies. I always provide a week's supply of the food the puppies have been fed on, so that if the new owners wish to change the method of feeding, this can be done gradually. Many breeders feed a milky cereal meal last thing at night. But you will notice that my final meal of the day for puppies is meat and biscuits. This is because I am aiming for my puppies to go through the night without having to pass water (urinate), and liquid late at night is a hindrance in this respect.

DIET SHEET: EIGHT WEEKS OLD
8.30am (Breakfast): 1/2 pint milk feed (2 oz to 1/2 pt of boiling water. Let it cool to blood heat).
lpm (Lunch): 6 oz meat (take the meat out of the refrigerator in plenty of time, so that it can be served at room temperature), plus 2 oz approx. of puppy biscuits, soaked in hot water. Mix the meat and biscuits together, supplementing with yeast (in tablet form) and calcium, according to the amounts instructed on packets.
5pm (Tea): Repeat breakfast.
9pm (Supper): Repeat lunch, without additives.

A well-balanced diet will keep your Golden healthy and happy.

A fit dog which does not become overweight will live longer.

GENERAL POINTS
1. Give your puppy a dog biscuit at 'goodnight time,' and always leave a supply of fresh, clean water available.
2. Gradually increase meat, so that at twelve to thirteen weeks, your puppy is getting 8oz at each meal. Cow or goat's milk can now be substituted for powdered milk.
3. When I change to fresh milk, I usually add a spoonful of honey to one of the milk feeds.
4. Gradually increase biscuits, so that at about thirteen or fourteen weeks your puppy is having approximately 5oz at each meal. At about this age, you can change from puppy biscuits to a small-bite biscuit.
5. Continue to feed four meals a day until your puppy is about 4 months old, and then drop the afternoon milk feed.
6. The next meal to cut out is breakfast, and I usually do this when the puppy is nine months old.
7. From now on, you will have to play it by ear as regards amounts. A puppy has a tremendous rate of growth between three months and twelve months, and you may well need to feed 3/4lb biscuits and 11/2lb meat, divided into two meals. When your dog is over twelve months of age, you can drop it back to approximately 1lb of meat and 1/2lb biscuits. The condition of the dog will tell you if you are feeding the right amount, and if in doubt, please ask the breeder.
8. When your dog is twelve months of age,you can, if you wish, feed the dog just one meal a day at about 6pm. Always try to feed at the same time each day. I, however, continue to feed my dogs twice a day, giving them about a third of the total amount at lunchtime, with the other two-thirds in the evening. Throughout the winter, all my dogs are given milk (slightly warmed) at breakfast time, with occasionally an egg added.
9. Cut out the yeast tablets in the summer, and the calcium supplement altogether when your dog is twelve months of age. Reintroduce the yeast tablets in the autumn through to April.

Chapter Three

THE NEXT STEPS

By the time your puppy is fourteen weeks old, the inoculations will have taken effect and the time has come to introduce your puppy to the big wide world.

LEAD TRAINING
Hopefully, during the eight to fourteen week isolation period you will have got the puppy used to wearing a small, lightweight collar with lead attached. Sometimes when you attach the collar the puppy sits down, puts the 'brakes on' and refuses to move. Do not drag it along, but hold a tidbit in your right hand, about two feet in front of the puppy's nose, and entice it to follow. Hold the lead in your left hand, and as the puppy's moves towards the 'goodie', let him feel the lead pull slightly. Repeat this procedure a number of times, occasionally giving the tidbit as a reward.

Another method is to hold the lead in your left hand (incidentally, the puppy must always walk on your left side), and get another member of the family to stand about ten yards in front of you, encouraging the puppy. Let the puppy pull towards the person, and repeat three or four times. Probably by now the puppy will be so keen to get to a favourite friend for the tidbit and hug, that it will already be forgetting about the lead attached to its collar. At this stage I do not mind the puppy pulling on the lead, but before this becomes a habit, the puppy must be taught to walk to heel as well as being taught to sit, stay and come.

THE FIRST OUTING
For the first trip off the premises, providing your puppy is reasonably proficient on the lead, I like to go for a short ride in the car (not just after a meal), and find a quiet spot where I can let the pup out for a *very short* walk on the lead. Hopefully, your pup will meet one or two friendly dogs, as the last thing you want is for the puppy to be upset by a bad-tempered dog on its first outing. The final trick is to get your puppy home without being car sick. Do not be disheartened if the pup is sick within fifty yards of arriving home – it often happens!

Very soon, your puppy will be so used to the car that it is a job to keep him out of it. You will also want to develop the exercise so that your puppy has a chance to run free. I always pick a spacious area that is safe with regard to traffic, for one of the problems you will more than likely encounter is that the puppy will not come to you whilst running free. If you have another dog in the house, take it with you so that when the old dog comes to you, the puppy will more than likely follow. Two golden rules on this subject are:
1. *Never* run after the puppy. The secret is to run away from the pup, preferably

ABOVE: The key to establishing a good relationship with your puppy is to be firm and consistent in training, and reward with plenty of praise.

RIGHT: Dogs of different ages require different amounts of exercise, and walks should therefore be tailored to suit individual needs.

LEFT: If you use a training aid, such as a glove or a toy, it will attract your dog's attention and help in establishing good heel-work.

BELOW: Goldens are an active breed and young, healthy dogs will require a period of free-running exercise every day.

towards the parked car and, more often than not, your puppy will come running after you, afraid of being left. If you have bought yourself a whistle, then while you are running away call and whistle at the same time. Three short sharp blasts: pip, pip, pip, repeated regularly mean 'come back to me at once'. If this is practised often enough, the puppy will soon return to you on whistle alone.

2. *Never chastise* your puppy when it eventually returns to you, or very soon it will relate coming to you with a good hiding. The opposite should be practised – lots of praise and lots of fussing.

PREPARATORY WORK

A puppy officially becomes a young adult or a teenager when it reaches the age of twelve months. At this age serious obedience and gundog training can begin, but until then there is a lot of preparatory work to be done, without boring your young puppy. I always believe in letting a Golden enjoy its puppy days, and any training I do is always on the basis of ' little and often.'

In these formative days, it is absolutely essential not to over exercise. No long tiring walks, either on or off the lead, but again 'little and often' with plenty of rest and sleep in between. Apart from socialising youngsters and acclimatising them to the outside world, my puppies do not go off the premises until they are six months old.

When you start to take your puppy out for regular exercise, it is a good idea to attach to its collar a disc, showing the dog's name along with your name, address, and telephone number, just in case it doesn't respond to your calling and whistling. The collar should be made of soft, rolled leather. Do not use a choke chain at this stage; these are used as a training aid later in life.

TEACHING MANNERS

One of the first things your puppy must learn is its name, and by using it as a preface to all instructions, or when putting its food down you will be amazed how quickly it gets the message. Similarly, the puppy can be taught to sit very quickly by gently pressing its bottom downwards as you give the command. The command "No" must be instilled in its mind from an early age, and is transmitted by the tone of voice in which it is given.

One of the first and most important things to learn when training, is that *a dog does not understand English.* I once saw an owner bawling and shouting the command "Sit" to a puppy, who had not the slightest idea what he was talking about. I pointed out to the embarrassed gentleman that if, at the same time he gave the command, he gently pressed down on the dog's back-end, all would be well – and it was.

JUMPING UP

Another bad habit, which requires nipping in the bud, is allowing your puppy to jump up at visitors. This should be stopped from the outset by the command "No", coupled with the action of actually putting the dog's feet back on the ground.

HEEL-WORK

I have mentioned elsewhere that I do not mind the puppy pulling while it gets used to walking on the lead. This practice, however, must be stopped at the earliest possible moment otherwise you could 'store up' a lot of trouble for the future. With the dog on your left hand-side, pull the lead sharply backwards until the dog is level with you, and couple this action with the command "Heel", given in a stern voice. Another method of counteracting this problem is to carry a second lead in your right hand, which you swing in a circle in front of the dog's nose as you both walk along. If your puppy moves too far ahead, then the swinging lead will gently touch its nose and make it move back into line.

Sometimes a young dog develops a nasty habit of pulling away, and sideways from you. This problem can be solved quite easily by walking along the side of a wall, so that the dog cannot pull away leftwards because of the wall, and cannot pull to the right because you are there yourself.

CHEWING
At about four to five months, a puppy will cut its new teeth, so, unless you want the furniture ruined, make sure your puppy has plenty of things to chew. When all the new teeth have arrived, check that none of the old ones are left (particularly the puppy canine teeth – fangs). If you have any doubts, let the vet have a look.

If you have followed the advice given in the book so far, then by the time your young Golden reaches its first birthday you should have a well-behaved, well-fed, well-groomed and an extremely contented and attractive dog.

ESTABLISHING A ROUTINE
When you are caring for a living creature, human or canine, it is essential to get into good habits so that you establish a balanced routine for you and your dog. There is no point being too ambitious in your plans, you must work out the routine of care – and fun – that will suit your lifestyle.

THE MORNING
My day starts about 6.30am when Judith (Linchael Alitalia of Carasan) aged ten, and Emma (Ch. Moonsprite Mermaid of Carasan) aged nine, who both sleep on the floor in my bedroom, decide its time for us to wake up – there is no need for an alarm clock at Carasan! We join the other dogs, who all sleep in the kitchen, where eventually milk and toast is served before exercise commences at 9am.

EXERCISE
At the present time, I have eight Goldens, each requiring different amounts of exercise, so they are usually taken out in three lots – never more than four at time. When deciding on the 'teams', I take several factors into account. The older dogs do not, obviously, require as much exercise as say a three-year-old, and a young nine-month-old puppy also needs limited exercise. I often find it is a good idea to take a couple of the old dogs with a young puppy, as they all require roughly the same amount of exercise, and the experience of the old ones soon rubs off on to the youngsters.

Morning exercise usually entails a trip in the car to the sand dunes (sometimes the beach), and consists of free running along the dunes for one mile, and free running along the promenade (hard surface) on our return to the car – a round trip of approximately two miles.

Back at home, the dogs go into the kennels, which have covered runs and outside

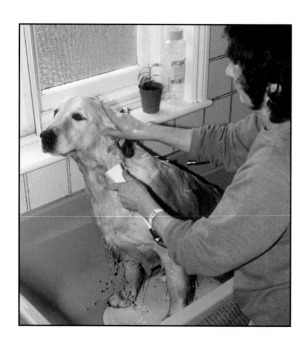

BATHING YOUR DOG

First wet the dog throughly. If your dog is in the bath, make sure you use a non-slip rubber mat.

Work the shampoo into a rich lather, being careful to avoid the dog's eyes, ears, nose and mouth.

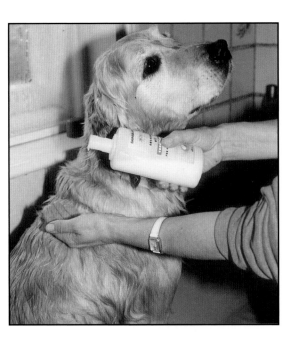

Apply the conditioner and leave it on for three minutes.

In warm weather the dog can be dried with a chamois leather and towels. In cold weather you will need to use a hair-dryer, making sure it is not turned up to too high a temperature.

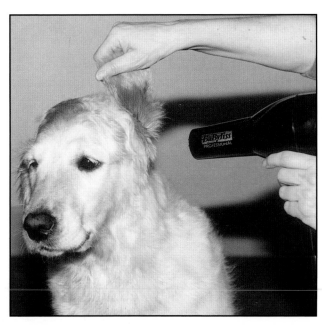

runs, both surfaces being made of concrete. The kennel floors are covered with sawdust and/or wood shavings, which are marvellous if the dogs have got dirty or wet while out on exercise. If, however, the dogs have been exercised in pouring rain, then they are always dried with a chamois leather (very good for soaking up the wet) and towelled, before being put in the kennels. The dogs do not normally sleep in the kennels, but if this is necessary, straw is added in the winter to the sawdust and shavings. We always make sure there is a constant supply of cold water available. In the summer the water tends to become warm, and so it is changed at regular intervals.

PREPARING FOOD
It is now time to make the food for the day, which consists of soaked 100 per cent wheatmeal biscuits, plus meat. The amounts vary, of course, for each dog, but as a guide an active young adult gets 1/2lb biscuits plus 1lb of meat. If I feed biscuits and meat together, I always soak the biscuits for one hour in hot water (with yeast extract added), before adding the meat. This is because I prefer the swelling of the biscuits to take place before entering the dog's stomach.

If you wish to feed hard biscuits, then feed them at lunch time and meat on its own in the evening, which can be in the form of canned meat (many varieties available), canned tripe, or raw black tripe available from firms which specialise in this type of product. When the preparation of the dogs' meal is completed, I add one garlic tablet (nature's antiseptic) ten yeast tablets (during winter months), and two teaspoonfuls of seaweed powder (aids coat and pigmentation).

The dogs receive one-third of the total meal prepared at around midday, and the rest at about 6pm. Of course, there are other methods of feeding but I, personally, think that complete feeds, although very nutritious, must become boring and uninteresting for the dog.

GROOMING
Before the lunchtime feed, all the dogs have to be groomed, and while this is being done, a daily inspection is carried out with regard to possible ear or skin problems. Most Goldens cannot wait for their turn to be groomed; they usually lie down while they are being groomed, which presents an ideal opportunity to check the feet and pads for any possible damage.

THE AFTERNOON
The afternoon is taken up with such things as trimming, bathing and various types of training.

BATHING
On the question of bathing, my dogs get bathed once a year, preferably in the garden on a lovely hot summer afternoon. If you have to bath your dog in the winter, it is better to use the bathroom, and put the dog in the bath, and use a shower appliance to wet the dog. Bathing is a two-handed job, and one-dog-per day is quite enough for anyone.

First of all, the dog is soaked to the skin with warm water, and then a proprietary dog shampoo is applied and worked into a rich lather. This should be completely rinsed off, before applying a special dog shampoo conditioner, which should be left on the dog for about three minutes. Now is the time to rinse, rinse, and rinse again with clean warm water, making sure all the conditioner and any of the original shampoo is out of the coat. Let the dog run round the garden, shaking itself, and then get to work drying it with a chamois leather and warm towels. Let the sun do the rest, while you continue to brush and comb the coat in the direction required. If you are bathing indoors, a hair-dryer is invaluable – but make sure it is not too hot for your dog.

EVENING
The dogs stay in the runs until about 4pm in the winter months, and then they are all taken for a short walk before coming into the house for the evening and night. At about 9.30pm they are taken out individually into the garden to perform their last 'duties'. In the summer they stay outside in the runs much later, before coming inside for the night.
So ends 'a day in the life' of the Carasan Goldens, and hopefully many of the procedures explained will be of help to the pet owner.

DO'S AND DON'T'S
1. DO be a responsible owner and pick up after your dog in public places.
2. DO get your dog used to having its feet wiped, before coming into the house.
3. DO put your dog on its collar and lead before opening the car door.
4. DO take the trouble to exercise your dog every day, yourself.
5. DON'T let your dog out of the house to run wild in the street.
6. DON'T let your dog out in the garden and expect it to exercise itself – it won't.
7. DON'T forget to follow the worming instructions for an adult dog (see Chapter 2).

THE VETERAN GOLDEN
Finally, please remember to care for your Golden as it reaches old age.
1. Keep your dog warm (old dogs do tend to suffer from rheumatism).
2. Watch your dog's weight (an old, fat dog is not a happy one).
3. Feed two meals instead of one large meal (the dog's digestive system will have deteriorated).
4. Do not over-exercise.
5. Do not neglect trimming and bathing, just because old age is approaching.

The wheel has almost gone full circle, and the dreaded decision of when to part with your old, ailing dog is at hand. Remember it is the interests of the dog that are of paramount importance, and a delay can cause much unnecessary suffering. Be guided by your vet, and when the moment arrives for him to give the single injection, pluck up the courage to be present so that your dog can die in your arms, hearing your voice.
I always have my dogs cremated, and I insist that I receive the correct ashes, in order that they can be buried under the tree in the garden.

Anatomy Of The Golden Retriever

1. Muzzle	**6. Croup**	**11. Brisket**
2. Stop	**7. Tail**	**12. Pastern**
3. Occiput	**8. Hock**	**13. Chest**
4. Withers	**9. Stifle**	
5. Topline	**10. Tuck up**	

Carasan Colonel, a typical show dog with good overall construction.

Chapter Four

STANDARD AND SHOW

The Breed Standard is a list of attributes which go into the making of the ideal Golden Retriever. The Breed Standard is drawn up by leading experts in the breed, and is published by a country's national Kennel Club. The Breed Standard may be differently set out from country to country, and there may be minor differences, but with Golden Retrievers we are fortunate in having a breed that has a 'universal' look. The Standard is used widely by breeders and judges in their quest for the 'perfect Golden' which, needless to say, has not yet been born.

INTERPRETING THE BREED STANDARD
The Breed Standard should be viewed as a blueprint, but it is obviously open to individual interpretation. If this was not the case, the same dog would always win in the show ring, and all dogs of that breed would look identical.

Everyone involved in a breed makes a particular study of the Standard, and I will give my interpretation of some of the more important features which will help you in choosing not only a lovely Golden pet, but a sound, nice-looking animal as well. Of course, it must be realised that there is a world of difference between a young puppy and a mature dog, but it is often said that an eight-week-old puppy is a miniature edition of the finished article.

GENERAL APPEARANCE
In trying to describe what a Golden Retriever should look like, it is important to bear in mind that his calling in life is that of a gundog. In order to jump a five-barred gate, carrying a pheasant, duck or goose, the Retriever must be strong, powerful and balanced. 'Balanced' is not an easy term to describe, but basically it means that everything must be in proportion – not too long, not too short, not too small, not too tall. In other words, the dog should be of correct height to balance its length.

The desired height for a Golden Retriever dog is 22-24 inches, according to the UK Standard, and 23-24 inches, according to the American Standard. A bitch should be 20-22 inches (UK); 21 1/2-22 1/2 inches (American). It is not always easy to be as specific with regard to weights. As a guide, the males in my kennel range from 70-80lb, and the bitches from 62-72lb. This is slightly heavier than the Goldens in America, where the Standard calls for males to be between 65-75lb, and bitches should be 55-65lb.

TEMPERAMENT
Perhaps the most endearing characteristic of a Golden is its temperament. A Golden

Retriever must always be kindly, friendly, intelligent, confident and biddable. Perhaps it would be helpful to explain what sort of confidence we are looking for? We expect a Golden to be confident, but certainly not over-confident. Amongst other things, we expect it to be a good house dog warning of intruders, but we do not expect it to be a guard dog – that would most certainly be out of character.

A biddable or eager dog is one that will do what it is told to do without question, and without the necessity of having to have the command repeated. Most Goldens will go to endless pains to please their owners at all times.

THE HEAD
One of the most beautiful features of a Golden Retriever is its head, with that kindly, melting expression, which applies to males as well as females. Everyone has their own interpretation as to what constitutes an ideal head, but one of the most beautiful I have ever seen is that of Linchael Alitalia of Carasan (pictured on page 40). A newcomer to the breed may well be asking "What is it about Alitalia's head that the author considers so outstanding?" My answer is firm and decisive, and can be described in two words: Balance and Expression. The balance of her head is well nigh perfect in that everything is in the proportion required. The beautiful, gentle, alert, inquisitive, and, yes, cheeky expression emanates from those dark-brown appealing eyes, with lovely dark rims.

A black nose is preferred, and it is 'icing on the cake' if it remains so. Some Goldens never loose their pigmentation (skin colour), others lose it, and then get it back. Such things as cold weather, or in the case of bitches, the hormone cycle can be responsible for the inconsistency with regard to pigmentation. The American Standard sensibly states that a dog should not lose marks in the show ring if its nose fades to a paler colour in cold weather.

SHOULDERS, TOPLINE AND STIFLES
It is worth trying to evaluate these parts of a dog's anatomy, as it is a great help when selecting a puppy. The shoulder blade and upper arm should be of equal length, with a 90 degree angle, thus placing the front legs well back under the body, with the elbows close fitting. This can be seen in the photograph of Carasan Colonel on page 36, which also shows correct shoulder/upper arm placement. The neck is long and muscular, and is in perfect proportion to the front assembly and rest of the body.

When considering the overall outline of the dog, a natural progression from the neck and shoulders is the topline. This should be completely level, with no dip in the middle, and no suggestion of any slope from back to front. The tail should be set on and carried level with the back, in other words, an extension of the topline. One of the most striking examples of this in recent years is my own Ch. Moonsprite Mermaid of Carasan (pictured on page 48).

This bitch has a superb, level topline, which is accentuated by the fact that the tail is held as a perfect extension. When the dog moves, its tail should be carried level with the back, and no curl at the tip should be evident. However, do not worry too much about this point when choosing your puppy, for at six weeks old the puppies will probably still be using their tails as an aid to balance, and so their tails will be carried at all angles, including straight up in the air.

One feature which will be evident in varying degrees, even at six weeks, is the correct bend of stifle and general rear angulation. One of the outstanding examples of this requirement is shown by Sh. Ch. Gyrima Solitaire (pictured on page 40), owned by Alan and Heather Morris of the Sandusky Kennel.

The photograph also shows the hind pastern (hock to foot) to be of correct angulation and length, and in perfect proportion to the bend of stifle. This relation of hock to stifle is described in the Standard as a 'well let down hock'. The hocks should be straight when viewed from the rear, neither turning in nor out.

One of the most undesirable features in this respect is what is known as 'cow-hocks'. When a dog is cow-hocked, its hocks point inwards, and some almost knock together when the animal is on the move. Here again, this is not a point to be too dogmatic about at the age of six weeks, as the puppy has only been on its feet for some two to three weeks, and will not yet have the desired strength which facilitates sound movement.

COAT AND COLOUR
This is probably the most controversial subject in the Golden Retriever breed, and it is the one subject where prospective purchasers of puppies have preconceived ideas. Whatever else their requirements, they are usually pretty definite as to the colour they want.

The UK Standard states: "Any shade of gold or cream, but neither red nor mahogany." The American Standard calls for: "Rich, lustrous golden of various shades," and an "extremely pale" or "extremely dark" colour is undesirable.

In any litter, there is often a range of colours. Obviously, if two pale Goldens are mated together, then there will probably be a preponderance of roughly the same colour, and likewise with the darker Goldens. This, however, is not always the case. I once mated a very dark dog to a dark bitch, and while the majority of the litter were the colour of their parents, one male was the palest colour imaginable.

The coat itself can be flat or wavy with profuse feathering, and it should have a dense water-resisting undercoat. Everyone has their own preference with regard to colour and coat texture, but a judge must put away personal preferences and adjudicate to the Standard. My own preference is for a mid-gold, with lighter coloured featherings. However, the colours in my own kennel range from pale cream to rich gold, and when I judge my selection usually follows the same pattern.

THE CHAMPIONS
As well as demonstrating the specific points mentioned, the dogs which I have referred to are also good examples of other desired attributes called for in the Standard when considering a fully-grown Golden Retriever. Each possesses the correct amount of bone (thickness of legs) and they have cat-like feet (not splayed). They are all beautifully balanced, with the corresponding depth of body, and being champions, they all have that indefinable requirement, known as quality or glamour.

You now have a rough idea of some of the more salient points to look for when going to choose your puppy, and what constitutes a typical looking Golden Retriever. Remember, the breeder will probably have had a lifetime's experience and will be an expert in the breed, so my advice is to be guided accordingly.

ON WITH THE SHOW
So you think you might want to show your dog? Nothing wrong with that, providing

LEFT: Linchael Alitalia of Carasan showing a beautifullly balanced head.

BELOW: Sh. Ch. Gyrima Solitaire showing correct bend of stifle and rear angulation.

The Golden Retriever comes in many different shades, and everyone has their own preferences. The paler colour is very popular in the UK but it would be faulted in the show ring in America. The more traditional 'golden' colour is more acceptable in America.

you go into the venture with your eyes wide open. Showing Golden Retrievers is very competitive, and as long as you do not expect instant success, then you may last longer than the average newcomer.

Before deciding finally whether or not you wish to start on a show career, I would strongly advise you to visit a local match meeting or small show in your area to make sure the life appeals to you. Your breeder will be able to tell you when and where these events are being held. If you like what you see, then order one of the dog papers, and you will find details of all the forthcoming shows. In the UK, the English Kennel Club has controlled dog shows and field trials since its formation in April 1873. The Kennel Clubs in America, Europe, Australia and New Zealand have not been in operation for as long as the English Club (the American Kennel Club was founded on September 17th, 1884), but in their own countries, they control the world of pure-bred dogs. Part of the control is the maintaining the records of the dogs who have been registered with them. Dogs can only be shown if they have been registered with their national Kennel Club (See Chapter 2).

TYPES OF SHOWS

BRITAIN
In the British dog papers you will see advertisements for various types of shows, the two most frequent being OPEN and CHAMPIONSHIP events.

OPEN SHOWS: These can be subdivided into General Open shows, and Breed Open shows. At General Open shows there are separate classes for many different breeds, including Goldens, and most breeds will have four or six classes and their own judge. Later in the show, variety classes are held and in these classes you get a chance to compete against other breeds and have the benefit of a 'second opinion' usually from a completely different judge.

At a Breed Open show you will only find Goldens present and one judge will usually officiate. At this type of show there will probably be around ten classes for each sex.

CHAMPIONSHIP SHOWS: These are the only shows where the Kennel Club Challenge Certificates can be won (the Kennel Club must approve the judges who award their Challenge Certificates). Three Challenge Certificates, or CCs for short, under three different judges make a Golden Retriever into a SHOW CHAMPION. For a gundog to become a FULL CHAMPION it must run and gain its qualifier at a field trial, or at a special breed qualifying day.

There are two types of Championship shows: All Breed Championship shows, and Breed (Golden Retrievers) Championship shows. At both these types of shows there is a wide classification for Golden Retrievers, and there will also be two judges, one for each sex.

AMERICA
MATCHES: The local All Breed and Specialty Clubs will probably hold one or two matches a year. These are advertised in the 'dog Press', giving details of breeds, classes and judges. Entries are made on the morning of the show. Judges are often aspiring to become Championship show judges. Classes usually range from Puppy

through Novice and on to Open. Sometimes the classes are for mixed sexes, or in the case of Specialty matches, most classes will be divided by sex. Champions are not eligible for matches.

CHAMPIONSHIP SHOWS: These can be all breeds, selected breeds, or one breed. They are advertised in the 'dog Press'. Premiums are sent to all intending exhibitors. After the closing date for entries, passes, catalog numbers and schedules will be sent to exhibitors. Points are awarded towards the Championship title by a judge who is approved by the Kennel Club. A total of fifteen points under three different judges must be gained for a dog to become a Champion, including two 'majors' under separate judges (3,4, or 5 point wins).

SPECIALTIES: These are held annually or bi-annually by the club concerned, usually attracting large entries. Again, Championship points are awarded. The judge is normally someone held in high esteem by breeders and exhibitors, and sometimes an overseas judge receives an invitation to officiate.

LEARNING TO SHOW YOUR DOG
Before you start entering serious competition, you must first become proficient in the art of presenting your dog and exhibiting it. The place to learn is at a club which holds special classes in ring training or 'ringcraft', and here you are taught to show your dog to its best advantage, and much valuable advice is given on all aspects of the dog game, in a friendly and enjoyable atmosphere.

TRIMMING
One of the things you will have to learn before your first show is how to trim your dog. Here again, the golden rule is 'little and often', and if this procedure is followed, then no major trimming will be necessary. Breed Clubs often hold trimming demonstrations, and you would be well advised to attend if at all possible. There are different types of scissors for trimming different parts of the dog, and you should seek advice as to which type you should purchase.

As a rough guide, the parts of a Golden that require trimming are: the ears and front neck, the chest (often referred to as the 'shirt-front'), sometimes the shoulders, the tail, the feet, the rear pastern (hock to foot), the back of the front pastern (stopper pad to front feet) and, finally, the nails often require cutting.

ENTERING A SHOW
The time has now come to send for the show schedule or Premium list which will include an entry blank, which must be filled in and sent off before the date of closing. Entering a show does not mean you have to attend, as many unforeseen things can happen to your dog (loss of coat, a bitch coming in season) between the closing date and actual show.

Pay attention to detail when filling in the form, and study the definitions of the various classes very carefully. Some classes are dependant on the dog's age, and others on what the dog has won. Keep a record of how many wins you have had in certain classes, because if you do not, you can rest assured some fellow exhibitor will know the exact total, and the last thing you want is to be reported for contravening the regulations – albeit inadvertantly.

Trimming the ears.

THE ART OF TRIMMING

Bernard Bargh shows how to trim a Golden Retriever for the show ring.

ABOVE: Bernard moves on to the chest or 'shirt-front'.

LEFT: The shoulders recieve attention.

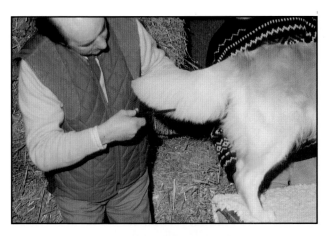

Great care is taken with the tail, which contributes to the overal balance of the dog.

The feet must be trimmed, cutting back the hair that grows between the pads.

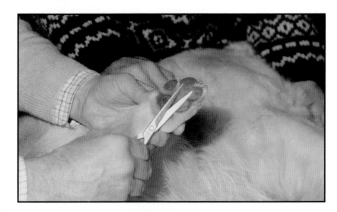

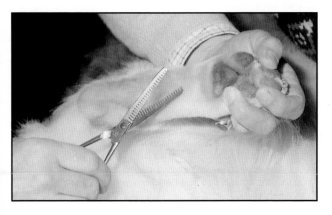

The rear pastern (hock to foot) must be trimmed, and this also applies to the back of the front pastern (stopper pad to front feet).

When filling in the entry form, print the details required so that no mistakes will appear in the catalogue, which you can buy on arrival at the show. Before posting the entry form, I always put the details clearly on the front of my schedule. Remember, the show can be anything up to two months ahead, and many are the exhibitors who have turned up with the wrong dog!

FINAL PREPARATIONS
The countdown to the show has now begun: regular exercise, regular grooming and regular practice are all the order of the day. Trimming must be completed no later than a week before the show, and any bathing necessary must be done at least two days before the show, otherwise you will find it almost impossible to get the coat lying in its proper position.

Having got the dog ready, spend the day before the show getting the car ready, packing a show bag, and packing your own bag. Everyone has their own ideas as to what they will need at a show – some look like they have arrived for a month's stay, and others turn up with a dog and a comb. In between the two is, of course, the ideal and my list, which I have on display in the office, (so I won't forget anything) includes:

DOG SHOW BAG
1. Ring Clip and Badges: In some locations the ring clip, a device used to hold the ring number on the exhibitor's atire, is required. You will often see exhibitors wearing badges, these are usually the breed clubs of which they are members and are for show; they have no relevance in the actual exhibiting of the dog.
2. Leather lead, benching chain, show lead: The leather lead and collar is for taking the dog to the show, the benching chain is to fasten the dog to the bench (nearly all Championship shows in the UK are benched) and, of course, the show lead is what the dog wears when being exhibited.
3. Comb and brush: For that last-minute preparation, while the preceding class is in progress.
4. Liver tidbits: Used by many exhibitors to get their dog to perform to its maximum potential. I usually boil the liver, let it cool and dry, and then cut it into small pieces.
5. Wet cloth in a plastic bag, talcum powder, and towels: The weather can be foul (and unpredictable in the UK), and no matter how careful you are, your dog can get very dirty before going into the ring. Always remember presentation can mean the difference between success and failure – it is after all partly a beauty contest!
6. Water, water dish, and food for the dog: I always take water from the tap in the kitchen, and plenty of it. The reason? I do not want the dog to get any stomach upset from drinking water that it is not accustomed to. Similarly, I prepare the dog's normal meal and take it to the show with me, and feed *after,* the dog has been in the ring. In the ring, I want the dog to concentrate on the liver I have prepared !
7. Bedding: This is for the dog to lie on next to the ringside, or to put on the bench. *Always* wash the bedding as soon as you return home, the last thing you want is to bring back germs or infections that your dogs at home could catch.
8. Schedule, correspondence sent to you by show authorities, and pen: The schedule is to remind you which class you entered; the show authorities will have sent you a ticket to get into the show, and you will need a pen to mark up the results of each class in the catalogue.

YOUR OWN BAG

Do not forget refreshment for yourself, plus an extra sweater, extra shoes, and wet weather gear. I also always make sure I have a 'survival kit' in the car, in case we break down miles from anywhere. While on the subject of cars, it is an offence to keep a dog in a car without proper ventilation, and if caught by the show authorities, it can result in unpleasant consequences for the thoughtless owner. Finally, before setting off for the show, remember the owner should look smart as well as the dog.

THE BIG DAY

The best piece of advice I can give you is: *Give yourself plenty of time.* I aim to arrive one hour before judging is due to start. I immediately let the dog relieve itself, and then get a seat round the ring with the dog on its bed by my feet, or put the dog on its bench, depending on the type of show. Many exhibnitors find a crate is a safe, comfortable place to keep dogs at a show.

You may wish to practise with your dog under actual show conditions before ring time. If you do, make sure their are no regulations against doing so. It is then back to the ringside seat, relax with a cup of coffee, and wait for it to happen.

JUDGING

What exactly is happening when a dog is judged? The judge is making a decision that one dog in the class is nearest to the 'ideal' dog, as described in the Breed Standard. After examining each dog, and comparing them mentally to the Standard, the dogs are then compared against each other and placed accordingly.

Judging dogs and interpreting the Standard is a bit like looking at a famous painting with a group of people; everyone views it differently – 'one man's meat is another man's poison!' A judge should not be swayed by the breeding of a particular dog, or by who owns it. If the judge's best friend has the worst dog, and his worst enemy has the best dog then, without question, the dogs must be placed accordingly. Quite naturally, a judge is bound to be attracted by the type of Golden he or she is trying to breed, and should not be criticised for selecting such dogs.

As you attend more shows and gain more experience, you will soon find out which judges like your particular type of dog and then naturally, if your dog is in good condition when these particular judges officiate, you will enter under them. Likewise, experience will teach you which judges are not completely honest in their awards; the answer then is to avoid them like the plague, and do not waste time, energy and money on them.

One of the main skills in judging is balancing good points and bad points. Hopefully, you will not show under what we call a 'fault judge' who discards every dog for its faults and ends up selecting a mediocre specimen with no great virtues, but has 'thrown out' a very typical dog, with only minor shortcomings

You may meet a judge who has a thing about one part of the anatomy, i.e. heads, feet, tail, or tail carriage, and he or she may well select a dog with a beautiful head but everything else is below standard. One other point to remember is that a wide range of colours are allowed in Goldens, but at some time you are likely to show under a judge who has a definite bias to a certain colour.

If it is not your dog's colour, then do not bother entering. The method of judging is more or less the same with all judges, although some do use small variations of their own.

ABOVE: Showing your dog can be fun, but do not expect instant success. Competition is fierce.

RIGHT: The art of posing your dog in the show ring.

RING PROCEDURE

Basically, when you enter the ring you will be given a ring number which you display in the customary manner. You then set up your dog in show stance as you will have been taught to do at the training classes. Give yourself plenty of room. There is no need to 'crowd' the dog in front, and do not let the one behind you get too close. The judge will now take a preliminary look at all the exhibits, and may ask everyone to move round the ring together with their dogs, ending up in the place from which you started.

The judge will now 'go over' (inspect) each dog individually, and ask you to move with your dog at a steady pace. This could either be up and down the ring in a straight line, twice (the second time the judge will move to the side to watch the lateral movement), or in a bigger ring you will be asked to move your dog once in a large triangle or "L" pattern.

When you have had your turn, let your dog relax a little. As soon as you see the last exhibitor's dog being gone over, then it is time for you to begin to set up your dog ready for the judge's final inspection. In a small class the judge will probably make the final choice immediately; in a larger class the judge will sometimes select several dogs and then from these pick the final winners.

In the UK, when the class in each sex has been judged, the ring steward will call for 'all unbeaten dogs', and if you have won your class and not been beaten in another, you are eligible to compete for the challenge certificate. Winners compete for Best of Breed, and that Golden has the honour of representing the breed in the Gundog Group, which is usually judged by a different judge.

In the United States, all undefeated class winners of each sex compete for Championship points. The best male and female compete for Best of Breed with any Champions entered. The winner of Best of Breed competes in the Sporting Group.

CONCLUSION

So your first show is over and, perhaps, it was not as frightening as you feared. Do not be too disappointed if you didn't do as well as you expected, remember tomorrow is another day, more than likely the same dogs will be placed in a completely different order by another judge. Be generous in defeat and congratulate the winner, for tomorrow you may be the winner, and the other exhibitors will, hopefully, be congratulating you.

Chapter Five

THE VERSATILE RETRIEVER

GUNDOG TRAINING

A Golden Retriever is a Gundog, and its job in the field, as its name implies, is to find and retrieve shot and wounded game tenderly to hand.

If, when you decided to buy a Golden Retriever puppy, your prime aim was for it to be used as a shooting dog, then it would have been wise to purchase from a working strain. Working lines are more biddable and trainable, because that is what they are bred for – they are, however, much more wiry in appearance than Goldens bred for the show ring. If you bought from a show breeder, then there is no need to worry, for all Golden Retrievers have the instinct to carry and retrieve, as you will have noticed, and hopefully encouraged, whilst your puppy has been growing up.

It is not possible, nor indeed desirable, in the space of this Chapter to go into the details of Field Trials and Working Tests. I will outline the basic principles of simple retrieving. If you then wish to proceed further, there are many advanced books on the subject, the most famous being *Gundogs (Training & Field Trials)* by P. R. A. Moxon, published by Popular Dogs. Equally informative, with special emphasis on the Golden Retriever, is a book called *The Complete Guide to the Golden Retriever* by Michael Twist, published by Boydell and Brewer. The working of Goldens in the USA is very popular, and many clubs run training classes and competitive events. The American Kennel Club offers many excellent booklets, the most useful being *Regulations and Guidelines for A.K.C. Hunting Tests for Retrievers.*

LESSONS FOR THE OWNER

"It's the owner who needs training, not the dog," so said John Halstead, the famous Gundog trainer. John's training classes, which I attended for some two years, were full of blunt, down-to-earth commonsense, which will repay study by aspiring trainers. The basic rules included:
1. Train little and often – half an hour, once or twice a day.
2. Patience is a virtue – do not take the dog out if you are in a bad mood.
3. You are ordering the dog, not asking it – the tone of your voice is all important.
4. Remember each dog has a different character – some need coaxing, others firm handling.
5. Get the dog to concentrate on *you* – if it is doing that, it won't be thinking about anything else.
6. Choose a completely quiet place for early training – the last thing you need is children or other distractions appearing at the vital moment.

7. Always stop on a high note – *you* will be happy and the puppy most certainly will be.

OBEDIENCE

Before any retrieving whatsoever is attempted, your puppy or young adult must be 100 per cent obedient to 'Sit', 'Stay', and 'Come' commands. When your dog is sent out for that first retrieve, it is imperative that the dog returns to *you* with its prize, and does not run off to the other end of the field, imagining that it is some sort of game.

As mentioned in Chapter 3, I like to start training at about twelve months, or possibly a little earlier, and, hopefully, by that age the puppy will be walking reasonably well on the lead. Unfortunately, 'reasonably well', as far as gundog training is concerned, is not good enough. The next step is walking to heel *off* the lead, and the more strict you are on the lead, the easier it will be off the lead.

WALKING TO HEEL ON THE LEAD, AND THE 'SIT'

For this I put the dog on a medium choke chain (not too heavy, not too light), with a leather lead. Walk along a quiet path with dog on left hand-side, and the lead held very loose. If the dog does not heel, tighten the choke chain sharply by a pull on the lead backwards, and a command of "Heel".

When this has been perfected, make the dog sit by a click of the choke chain, at the same time raising your open right hand saying "Sit". Eventually, after the command "Sit", you can give one long blast on your whistle. After three or four short training sessions you will find that the dog will sit for either a click of the choke chain, a raised right hand, a command of "Sit", or a long blast on the whistle. When out shooting, it is the whistle or raised hand that is used for this command, for if everyone shouted "Sit", it would almost certainly disturb the game in the vicinity.

WALKING TO HEEL OFF THE LEAD

Walk ahead with dog on choke chain and lead, and suddenly drop the lead on the floor. Keep walking, and you will be amazed to find that your dog continues to walk to heel, as though nothing has happened.

The next step is to remove the lead from the choker altogether, and walk along, at first with your finger in the choker hole, letting the dog know you have a certain amount of control. If everything is going to plan, gently remove your finger and keep walking, and before long you will be able to remove the choke chain altogether. At all times, you must encourage the dog to heel, and to pay attention to you by tapping your left thigh with your left hand.

THE 'STAY'

To teach your Golden to stay, sit your dog off the lead, facing away from home. Back off for about four yards with right hand raised, saying "Sit", then return and praise. Repeat, backing off a bit further, return and praise. The reason for the dog sitting facing away from home is that when you back away, the dog will be less likely to move towards you, than if it thought you were backing away towards home.

'COME'

As soon as you consider your puppy is steady enough in the 'Sit' position, and you

TEACHING YOUR DOG TO 'COME'

1. Give the command to 'Wait'.

2. Leave your dog.

3. Use the hand command to keep your dog in the 'Stay', and repeat the command "Sit", if necessary.

4. Call your dog, using the dog's name as an added incentive.

5. Finish with the dog in the 'Sit'. Reward with plenty of praise.

The choke chain must be used with the chain running through the top of the ring, so that it releases immediately.

can retreat without the dog moving, you can now think about calling your dog to you. The procedure is to sit your dog, again facing away from home, back away some twenty yards with hand raised, repeating occasionally the command "Sit." Walk all the way back to your dog, praise, and repeat the procedure a second time. Walk away for a third time, stop, face the dog, and call the dog to you, using its name and, with luck, the dog will come bounding to you.

Soon, you can introduce three short blasts on the whistle: Pip Pip, Pip, as well as calling by name. Finally, repeat a fourth time, and on this occasion walk back to the dog. You will notice you have called your dog to you only once in four exercises, so alleviating the danger of the dog anticipating your call. In this exercise, you used the dog's name for the first time, the reason being that we saved up this little treat until the moment you wanted the dog to run at speed towards you.

After about two weeks (fourteen half-hour sessions), you should have a young dog who will sit, stay, and come to you on verbal, or whistle command. Remember each dog is an individual, and some may take longer to get the message than others.

RETRIEVING
Once the Obedience training has been perfected, I find teaching the actual retrieving comparatively easy for, after all, that is what a Golden has been bred for.

I always start the retrieving practice in a restricted area, just in case the puppy decides to forget all it has learnt in the preceeding Obedience lessons. The ground I use for the first few lessons is 100 yards long, with gates at each end, and 10 yards wide, with a hedge on either side. For the first retrieve, I use a small lightweight, green canvas dummy (purchased from any decent gun shop), which I take to the training ground in my pocket.

I repeat *exactly* the procedure adopted when teaching the dog to stay, i.e. sit the dog off the lead facing *away* from home, back off for about four yards with right hand raised, saying "Sit." You are now facing the dog, standing four yards in front, with hand held up telling the dog to sit. Suddenly, out of your pocket, produce the dummy and throw it backwards over your shoulder, at the same time making sure the dog does not move.

Return to the dog, wait for a few seconds, and then send the dog for the dummy. The moment the dog's head goes down, shout its name and use your whistle to encourage the dog to return. Then, gently take the dummy from the dog's mouth, saying "Dead", and give much praise. You will have noticed that we threw the dummy *away* from home, the idea being that when the dog returned with the dummy, it was going *towards* home, so encouraging the dog to return to you.

Assuming the first retrieve was successful, I like to call it a day and finish on a high note for both owner and dog. Space does not allow a detailed description of all the variations, suffice it to say that soon you will be able to stand by the dog's side instead of in front, move out of the restricted area and, of course, longer and longer retrieves will be possible.

GAME RETRIEVES
After a few retrieves with the canvas dummy, I progress to using a rabbit dummy, which is slightly bigger and heavier. Basically it is a cured rabbit skin, stuffed with various items to the desired weight, and then stitched up. This serves as the dog's first introduction to fur, which I find especially helpful, bearing in mind that its first

retrieve of game will be a rabbit. After the rabbit retrieve, I let the dog retrieve a hen pheasant, and if the dog is not too keen to pick it up, I go back to the green canvas dummy, with the wings of the pheasant wrapped round it. Once the dog retrieves that, go back to a new hen pheasant, and there should not be any further problems. You will have noticed, so far, we have been using cold game, and usually it is but a short step to the dog becoming proficient at retrieving newly-shot game. In the United States, Golden Retrievers are usually not used on rabbits. If you would like your Golden to work on both fur and feather, remember that you must avoid confusion for the dog if you plan on any competitive work in the American format.

GUNFIRE
A Retriever should regard the sound of a shot as of no consequence whatsoever; it must never become a signal for a dash out to retrieve, neither should a dog be gun-shy. However, in the early days of training quite a few dogs are 'gun-nervous', and there is a vast difference between the two.

Providing a puppy gets used to distant bangs and loud noises from five weeks, when its hearing becomes acute, you rarely encounter any problems. As the puppy is growing up, I often fire my starting pistol, equipped with blanks, while the pup is feeding, first at a distance, and then getting nearer and nearer, as the dog gets older. At a later date, I change to my 12 bore, again fired at an ever decreasing distance.

OBEDIENCE COMPETITION

The Obedience taught to your puppy, in conjunction with its retrieving, will be of great help if you decide to go in for general Obedience. There are many training clubs to choose from, and Goldens have proved that they excel in this field.

BRITISH TITLES
In the UK, you will first join a class for Special Beginners, and will then progress as far as you can go through the different classes. If you wish to go in for competitions, the classes are: Beginners, Novice, Class A, B, C, and Championship C. Before progressing up the ladder you must gain the necessary qualifications in the previous class. You are given points for each exercise, and in Beginners, for example, the exercises include: Heel on Lead, Heel free, Recall from sit or down, Retrieve an article, Sit (one minute) handler in sight and Down (two minutes) handler in sight.

To date, there have been six Obedience Champions in the UK.

AMERICAN TITLES
In the USA Golden Retrievers take part in Obedience Trials, which are an examination in the basics of all forms of dog training. Behind each exercise there is a reason formulated as a result of generations of experience in training and working dogs. The importance of Obedience training is to teach the dog that it must obey at all times. Obedience Trials are divided into classes or grades of competition. Beginners compete in the Novice Classes A & B, and when a dog has won passing scores of 170 or more, at three shows, under three different judges, it gains the title of Companion Dog and the letters CD go after its name.

After further training, the dog moves upwards into the Open Classes A and B, and after it has won passing scores at three shows in these classes, the dog gains the title

THE RETRIEVE

When your dog has become more experienced you can throw the dummy when your dog is sitting at your left handside.

Most Goldens are only too keen to run out and fetch the dummy.

A well-trained dog returns immediately to the handler – overcoming any obstacles it encounters.

Jacko of Norwich in action retrieving a pheasant. When your dog is working well with dummy retrieves, you can progress to using game.

Companion Dog Excellent or CDX. Following more training, a dog may enter the Utility Class. This class may be divided into A and B classes, depending on the size of the event (the Utility A Class being for dogs who have not previously won the UD title). Three scores of passing or better, earn the title UD. This is the highest title a dog can win, except a 'T' for Tracking or a 'TDX' for Tracking Dog Excellent. The dog's title then becomes Utility Dog Tracking (UDT) or Utility Dog Tracking Excellent (UDTX). Tracking tests are not held at dog shows, since they must be run out of doors.

To win Obedience titles there are certain qualifications, e.g. perfect score in each class 200, passing score 170. But no dog can qualify for a 'leg' towards its title, unless it has scored more than fifty per cent of the points allowed for each exercise of the competition. In the Novice Classes A and B, the tests and scores for a perfect performance are:

1. Heel on leash and figure eight	40 points
2. Stand for examination off leash	30 points
3. Heel off leash	40 points
4. Recall	30 points
5. Long sit (1 minute)	30 points
6. Long down (3 minutes)	30 points

MAXIMUM TOTAL SCORE 200 POINTS

AGILITY
Since the widespread coverage on television of the UK's Crufts Dog Show, Agility has become more popular than ever. It is gratifying to note that Golden Retrievers are reaching the highest level in this sphere. A number of detailed books on general dog agility are available from most libraries and large bookshops.

OTHER ROLES
Golden Retrievers fulfil many other roles than those already mentioned. Probably they are best known, all over the world, as Guide Dogs for the Blind. Many Goldens are also Hearing Dogs, helping deaf people. They also work as Therapy Dogs, visiting people in hospitals and homes for the elderly. Golden Retrievers are in great demand as 'sniffer' dogs, detecting drugs and explosives, which is not surprising since they possess such a marvellous sense of smell.

Chapter Six

BREEDING

My advice to the pet owner with regard to breeding is – *do not*. Indeed, I find it difficult to think of one good reason why you should decide to mate your bitch. The reasons, however, for *not* mating are legion.

TO BREED OR NOT TO BREED
First of all, let us get rid of the old chestnut that it does a bitch good to have at least one litter. This viewpoint is absolute rubbish, and there is no scientific proof whatsoever in the statement – you may as well say that every woman should have a baby!

Remember, breeding is for the specialist, not for the amateur. If you have any preconceived ideas that you will make some money out of the litter to pay for that holiday abroad, then forget that one too. I recently had an enquiry from a pet owner who wanted to use one of my stud dogs, and naturally I asked why they wanted to mate their bitch. "To make some money," came the reply – my answer is not printable!

Unfortunately, another stud dog owner is always likely to oblige, and into the world, some nine weeks later, come eight or nine poor innocent puppies, some of whom will probably join the ranks of unwanted dogs, and will mean extra work and heartache for the rescue services, which do such a marvellous job.

It is more than feasible that you could lose money by breeding a litter. Consider the expenses involved in the preparation, expensive equipment that will be needed, hereditary certificates for the bitch, stud fee, vet fees, extra food for the mother and prospective litter, and numerous other incidentals which can add up to an appreciable amount. Then, horror of horrors, your lovely little girl produces two puppies!

However, let us assume that you are geared to the actual birth, you know what you are doing, and your bitch produces a normal-sized litter of seven or eight puppies. Having spent the past nine weeks looking after the in-whelp bitch (no going on holiday during this period) you now face a further eight weeks hard labour, and make no mistake, that is what it is. Do not think you can leave it all to the mother, because at about three weeks she will have had enough, and gradually during the fourth week you will be preparing five meals per day, every day for eight puppies – and mother will have stopped cleaning up after them!

Another important point to consider is whether you will be able to sell your puppies. Will those friends who said they wanted a pup, still want to take delivery, or will you be involved in unexpected expensive advertising, or worse still, will you

It is a myth to think that every bitch needs to have a litter in order to lead a full and happy life.

The Guide Dog for the Blind Association's success rate in producing good, working dogs is the result of a carefully controlled breeding programme.

have some of your puppies still eating you out of house and home at twelve weeks? You will not, at this stage, have the advantages of an established breeder who probably has a long waiting list, prior to the litter being born. Breeders in this position will probably be listed on a breed club puppy register, or will have other breeders passing enquiries on to them. In my experience, most pet owners who decide to let their bitch have 'just one litter' utter two immortal words as the last puppy goes off to its new home – NEVER AGAIN!

I have assumed, that if you are interested in getting involved in breeding, you own a bitch. However, my advice for the pet owner of a male, as regards breeding, is exactly the same – DON'T! As a pet owner, it is unlikely that your young male will ever be in demand for stud purposes, as this usually only comes from having success in the show ring.

By using him at stud once, you will have whetted his appetite, and this could store up untold problems for the future, including your dog wandering off in search of lady friends at every opportunity. Far better to work on the principle of 'What he's never had, he will never miss!'

If, despite the above warnings, you are still determined to go ahead and mate your bitch, I will endeavour to make the exercise as painless as possible for you by explaining in a step-by-step approach to the fundamentals involved. It is not possible, nor indeed desirable, to 'blind you with science'. For more detailed help and information, ask the person who bred your bitch.

WHAT AGE TO MATE?
The first point to establish is at what age should you mate your bitch? Most bitches come in season twice a year, and the popular view is that the third season is the ideal time for the first mating, although not much before the age of two years. At the other end of the scale, you cannot now, in the UK, mate a bitch of eight years or older, as the Kennel Club will refuse to register the puppies.

On the question of the latest age for a bitch to have her first litter, consider the fact that if you leave it until the bitch is six years old, it would be the equivalent of a woman having her first baby in her forties – not very desirable. The longer you leave the first mating, the more the risk of an unsatisfactory result, and I would not want to leave it much after three-and-a-half years of age.

Before mating, your bitch will have to be certified clear of the hereditary eye conditions, hereditary cataract and progressive retinal atrophy, and most stud dog owners will want you to have your bitch's hips X-rayed. If the score is very high, permission to use the stud dog may be refused. Others will be satisfied by the fact that you have had the hips X-rayed and scored, and will not be too perturbed by the actual score, providing it is not too horrendous.

BREEDING PROGRAMMES
Experienced breeders spend months, even years, in trying to decide which stud dog to use on their bitch. Their aim is to produce stock of similar type, but hoping to correct at least one fault the bitch possesses, while retaining all her virtues. The methods breeders adopt are line breeding, in-breeding and out-crossing. Before discussing these three terms, it is important to bear in mind that the aim of breeding any livestock is to breed an animal with qualities as good, or better, than those of the sire and dam.

IN-BREEDING
This is the mating of brother to sister, father to daughter, and mother to son, and should be avoided by the novice at all costs. This method cannot produce faults that are not carried by the original stock, nor can it produce virtues that are not already there in the first place. In-breeding, therefore, exaggerates both good and bad, and although it can produce superb specimens, it can also be the source of many disappointments. It is best left to the expert, who will have many years experience concerning the strains in question.

LINE BREEDING
This is in-breeding in a moderate form, and consists of matings such as half-brothers to half-sisters, with the common parent being an outstanding animal. Grandmother to grandson, grandfather to granddaughter, uncle to niece, aunt to nephew, and varying degrees of cousins, are other examples of this method.

Line breeding condenses the plus points of a family, and by selection and the occasional outcross, a breeder can improve his stock in type, quality, temperament, and other desirable features, as well as eliminating various faults that a particular line possesses. The prerequisite of any success in this field is the pedigree, and more importantly, the understanding and knowledge of the various animals detailed in it.

OUT-CROSSING
This is the equivalent of taking a shot in the dark – it is the mating of completely unrelated animals. Sometimes, of course, this method is used on purpose to bring in some outside blood, and in the first generation can prove reasonably satisfactory. However, if practiced on a regular basis, it can be the path to disaster. The novice breeder who uses 'the dog down the road' will have almost certainly used an outcross, as it is most unlikely that the dog in question will be bred the same way as your bitch.

CHOOSING A STUD DOG
If we so-called experts are sometimes in a quandary as to which stud dog to use, what hope is there for the novice? I can simplify the answer with one 'don't' and one 'do':

DON'T take the easy way out and use the Golden who lives down the road, or one you met while out exercising. The odds are he will probably have never been used at stud, and, therefore, he will not know what to do. Equally, he is highly unlikely to be in possession of the necessary hereditary health certificates, and if you have gone to all the trouble and expense of getting certificates for your bitch, it would be an extremely silly move to ignore this aspect.

DO contact your breeder, who will be only too pleased to suggest a father. Most probably the breeder will have kept a bitch out of the same litter as yours, and will, therefore, already have done all the thinking for you.

It is also worth asking the breeder for a second choice of stud dog, in case for some reason the mating with the original dog is not successful. The second choice may be many miles away from the original one (the bitch always travels to the stud dog), but if you are serious in your aims then the effort will, hopefully, be well

Your bitch must be free from hereditary defects if you plan to breed.

worthwhile. Sometimes the owner of your original choice will have another stud dog which he may try and persuade you to use. Do not agree to this, for if you had wanted to use the dog in question, he would not have been your second choice.

THE IN-SEASON BITCH
Once you have selected your stud dog, your first task is to make absolutely sure that you do not miss your bitch coming in season and, believe me, that can be very difficult indeed. Hopefully, when your bitch was last in season, you noted a rough order of events, and you will, by now, know the approximate time you expect her to be on heat. Generally speaking, before coming in season a bitch begins to grow her new coat, and she is often two-thirds in coat when she comes on heat. The idea being that in another nine weeks, when the puppies are born, she will be in full coat – nature's way of keeping them warm.

Before the actual season commences, bitches usually show a number of behavioural changes, such as increased frequency of urination, often combined with

Take your time to choose a reputable stud dog to complement your bitch.

the marking of territory, constant licking of the vulva, where there is often evidence of a white mucus which changes to a dirty-brown discharge.

These symptoms can last for a number of days, or weeks, and great care must be taken to notice when the dirty-brown discharge changes to the bright red blood, which can be seen on her feathers and also dripping on to the floor. To make things more complicated, some bitches show none of the above signs and simply, without warning, start dripping blood, which goes to show that you have to be observant at all times.

As soon as I know the bitch is in season, I worm her, unless I have recently done so in my strict worming regime. I always make sure my bitch is free from worms before mating, but the puppies always seem to be full of them. The reason for this is that the release of hormones during pregnancy activates roundworm larvae, which are dormant in the tissues of the bitch. These larvae are passed on to the unborn puppies, and by the time the puppy is two weeks old, the larvae have developed into adult worms. The only way to counteract this problem is to worm the bitch *after* she has become pregnant, and although there are proprietary brands of wormers available for this purpose, I have not yet had the courage to try one, for fear of complicating the pregnancy.

WHEN TO MATE?

Having already received permission, agreed terms, and notified the stud dog owner that your bitch is in season, the next big hurdle is to arrange the mating on the correct day – not an easy task – and even the most experienced breeder regularly gets it wrong. Hopefully, the following guidelines may be of help.

The first golden rule is to mark on your calendar the exact date that you first saw the bright-red blood, and for the next twenty-one days, great care must be taken that no unwelcome canine friends visit the premises. There are no hard and fast rules as to which day your bitch will be ready for mating. The variations are enormous: some may be ready at day seven, others at day seventeen, but the most common time is between the ninth and fourteenth day, with perhaps the twelfth day being the favourite.

I once read a marvellous article in which the following was printed in capitals: "THE RIGHT DAY FOR MATING IS WHEN THE BITCH SAYS IT IS THE RIGHT DAY, AND IT WILL NOT NECESSARILY BE THE SAME DAY AS IT WAS THE LAST TIME SHE WAS IN SEASON."

An old rule-of-thumb method to tell if a bitch is ready, is to wait until the vaginal bleeding has stopped, or turned to a straw colour. The trouble with this is that a number of bitches bleed throughout the twenty-one days. If you have more than one bitch, you will find that the one in season will 'stand' for the other bitch, and encourage it to mount her. This is another sign that the time is getting nearer, but it is not foolproof as your bitch may be prepared to let her female companion mount her, but she may not be ready to tolerate a dog.

One of the most commonly practised methods of 'guessing' the correct time is to rub your hand on the bitch's 'pants' (the feather around the vulva) and if her tail turns to one side, she should soon be ready. A more scientific way of determining the right day is a method called cytology, which entails the vet taking smears from the bitch's vagina at regular intervals, and examining the progression under a microscope. When *the* day is predicted, the bitch will have to be mated within twelve to twenty-four hours.

THE MATING

Before you set out, you have one last chance to change your mind about mating your bitch, so be absolutely certain that you want to go ahead with the project. Having decided to proceed, make sure your bitch is on a collar and lead, and when in the close vicinity of your destination let her relieve herself by passing water. Try and relax and place yourself in the hands of the stud dog owner, who will probably be very experienced, and will have his own particular way of managing his dog with regard to the mating.

The first thing to do on arrival is to exchange the various certificates. You will want to see the dog's eye, hip and registration certificates, and the stud dog owner will want to inspect your bitch's papers.

From experience, I have found that some owners do not want to be present at the mating, while others bring the whole family, including children. I like to have a maximum of three people present, one, probably the owner of the bitch holding the bitch's head, another person in charge of the middle to make sure the bitch does not sit down at the vital moment, and then the most important person of all, the one who works the stud dog. I like the mating to take place in a clean, spacious and enclosed area – a large well-lit garage is ideal.

The two animals are introduced to each other on collar and lead. If they appear to respond favourably to each other, I like to let them have a few moments of foreplay. Very soon, assuming it is the right day, the dog will mount the bitch and the mating will take place culminating, hopefully, in a tie. A tie is when the bulbous gland at the base of the penis swells and is held in the bitch by her constrictor muscle, thus both dog and bitch take an active part in this. The tie can last from five to forty-five minutes, and in extreme cases even longer. Although it is always preferred that a tie takes place, it is not essential for a successful mating.

POST-MATING
On completion of the proceedings, give your bitch a small drink of water and put her back into the car, without allowing her to urinate, and allow her to rest before the journey home.

Now is the time to attend to some more paperwork. First of all you must pay the stud fee, and in return receive a stud receipt. Should your bitch not conceive, most stud dog owners offer a free mating to the *same* bitch, within a twelve month period. You should also receive a Kennel Club form, signed by the stud dog owner, showing the dog's registered name, registration number and the date on which the mating took place. After the puppies are born, and if you wish to register them, you will fill in their names on this same form and forward it to the Kennel Club. The stud dog owner will also give you a copy of the dog's pedigree, eye certificate and hip score sheet.

In the United States the owner of the bitch must register the litter with the AKC. Each puppy will be issued an individual registration application, which goes with it when it is sold.

Although the mating has been successful you may, if the stud dog is free from other duties, be offered a further mating to try and make sure your bitch becomes pregnant. As the sperm will stay alive in the bitch for some forty-eight hours, it is best to miss a day before returning for a second mating. If the stud dog shows no interest, it is more than likely that the bitch will have passed her peak, and the one mating will have to suffice.

One word of warning, be very alert for the rest of the twenty-one days your bitch is in season. Take care not to let her near other male dogs, as the dog down the road may consider your bitch is still on heat.

Chapter Seven

WHELPING AND REARING

Once your bitch has been mated, there is no need to change her routine for the next four weeks. Continue to give the bitch plenty of exercise, in order to keep her in good muscular condition which will make the eventual whelping much easier. Keep the food ration exactly the same, but right from the beginning I add calcium to the diet, which comes in various forms and should be administered as per instructions.

DETECTING PREGNANCY
The usual period of gestation is nine weeks or sixty-three days, and for the first three weeks it is very difficult to ascertain whether your pride and joy is in whelp. Such things as morning sickness, the vulva remaining enlarged, the bitch becoming lethargic, and becoming more affectionate towards you than normal, are all possible signs that she is pregnant.

Some breeders do not bother to find out whether the bitch is in whelp or not; they just let nature take its course, and by about six weeks they will know, almost for certain, as by that time the teats should have become enlarged and pink in colour. I must say, I like to know as soon as possible if the bitch is in whelp. The reason for this is if I know she is definitely in whelp, then I can begin to increase her food, from about five weeks, and also start the laborious job of making all the preparations for the big event.

Providing you have a top-class vet, there is one sure-fire way of knowing whether your bitch is going to produce that hoped for litter. Between the twenty-sixth and thirty-first days of pregnancy, it is possible by palpation (feeling) to determine pregnancy in a breed such as the Golden Retriever. At this time, the foetuses will have reached 2.5-3.5cm (1-1 1/2in) in diameter, and they are in a position that enables the vet to make an accurate diagnosis.

The most reliable indication of pregnancy, other than by palpation, is evidence of a mucoid, very viscid, secretion at the vulva from approximately the thirty-second day which lasts almost until whelping. A bitch showing no such discharge is unlikely to be pregnant, and one showing it as late as the forty-second to forty-ninth day is more likely to be coming to the end of a false pregnancy.

THE IN-WHELP BITCH
Having ascertained your bitch is in whelp, she can now have her diet slightly altered and the planning for the rest of her pregnancy can be organised. At this stage I begin to get together all the items I will require for the actual whelping.

From about five weeks, I give milk, plus a whipped egg for breakfast. I gradually increase the bitch's meat (protein) ration to between 1 1/2 and 1 3/4lb a day, and the soaked biscuits (carbohydrate) to 1/2lb per day. This is divided into two or three meals, so as to make sure the bitch does not feel too uncomfortable. Great care should be taken to see that your bitch does not get too fat, as this can lead to difficult whelpings often due to oversize puppies. During this period, I add raspberry leaf tablets (to aid actual whelping), multivitamin tablets, and sterilised bonemeal to the diet.

Most bitches continue to eat like horses until the big day, others go completely off their food. Do not worry if your bitch will not eat, as the puppies from such a bitch will more than likely end up the same size as those from a bitch that has eaten her 'head off'.

As far as exercise is concerned, I try to keep to the normal routine for as long as possible. However, as the bitch gets bigger during the last two weeks, exercise is restricted, and from about six weeks, the car is 'out of bounds'.

WHELPING QUARTERS
One week before the due date, I get the whelping quarters completely ready. Goldens normally whelp on time, but occasionally the unexpected happens, and the last thing you want is 'panic stations'.

The first and most important decision you now have to make is where you wish your bitch to give birth to the puppies. If she is a house dog, which she most definitely should be if you only own one Golden, then it is lunacy to banish her to an outside kennel. A bitch should be permitted to whelp in her normal environment, and failure to allow this can cause untold problems, including a delay in first-stage labour. An ideal place for the whelping to take place is in the kitchen, or in a bedroom which is not in normal use, and then about four weeks after whelping everything – box, puppies and mother – can be moved to an outside kennel.

Here, at Carasan, circumstances are a little different, but the same principles apply. My bitches whelp in my office, and when the puppies are just over four weeks old, they are transferred outside to a kennel and run. The office is situated next to my garage, and the bitches spend many hours of their normal life 'helping' me with paper work, and so they are fully accustomed to the surroundings.

A week before the due date, I notify the vet of the precise date the litter is expected, and my office becomes the equivalent of a hospital ward with the following items very much in evidence:

WHELPING BOX
This is 44in square with a height of 20in. The front part of the box should be left open, but two individual boards of 44in x 6in and 44in x 12in should be available to slot in this space as the puppies become more active, but are not yet at the stage to be transferred outside. Around the three sides of the box, which are a fixture, should be fitted a rail to prevent the bitch crushing the puppies in the early days. The rail should be about 5in from the side of the box and 5in up from the floor. The whole box should be painted with a gloss finish so as to facilitate easy cleaning.

DULL-EMITTER INFRA-RED LAMP
I suspend the lamp approximately 3ft high, and slightly towards the side and corner of the box, so as to allow the bitch to keep out of the heat, yet leaving the puppies

under the lamp. It is most important this item of equipment is checked to be in working order before the puppies are born.

FLEECY POLYESTER FABRIC
This is marketed under a variety of trade names. It is highly absorbent, easily washable, and has the advantage of allowing the moisture to go through the material leaving the surface dry. This allows the puppies to keep warm, and its fluffy surface is a great aid when the puppies eventually start to crawl. Ideally, you should have three pieces cut to the size of the box, so that you can have one in the box, one in the washer and one in readiness.

Incidentally, I always line the floor of the whelping box with newspapers before putting in the bedding, the reason being that when the puppies urinate the surface of the bed remains dry, but the newspapers become soaked, thus making cleaning much easier. I also like to whelp the bitch on this material, and for this purpose I save up one or two old pieces which can be discarded when all the puppies have arrived.

CARDBOARD BOX
I always have a cardboard box, about 17in x 14in, fitted with a small piece of bedding, in case the puppies already born need moving for a short time. The box is put under the lamp and in full view of mother, in case she panics at the thought of losing her newly born. The cardboard box also comes in useful at a later date when the daily cleaning of the whelping box takes place.

GENERAL ITEMS
Plenty of newspapers, old towels, bucket, soap, cloths, disinfectant, thermometer (to test the bitch's temperature, prior to whelping), cotton wool (cotton), scales (to weigh the puppies), flashlight, sterilised surgical scissors (to cut the cords, if necessary) mild solution of iodine (to stem bleeding after cutting cords) cold milk, glucose and honey (for feeding the bitch during whelping), Milk of Magnesia (a help with fading puppies), simulated bitch's milk (in case of a very large litter), some brandy (not for you, but for the bitch) and a thermos for yourself.

THE WHELPING
SIGNS TO LOOK FOR
You will need to know when the whelping is imminent, and there are a number of signs you can be on the lookout for. During the final week of pregnancy, I cover the floor of the whelping box with newspapers and normally, as the week progresses, the bitch will start scratching at the papers in an effort to make a nest ready for her babies.

In the last twenty-four hours she will become restless; she will probably go off her food and pant a lot. After panting and shivering, she may drink a lot of water and then immediately vomit it up, this exercise being regularly repeated. She will pass water more regularly, and have many more motions than normally is the case.

The most reliable guide to impending birth is a marked, but fleeting drop in rectal temperature. I start taking the bitch's temperature twice a day one week before the due date. The normal temperature during this period is 100 degrees Fahrenheit (not 101.5 degrees Fahrenheit, which is the normal temperature for a healthy dog), but once the big drop to 97–99 degrees Fahrenheit occurs, then first-stage labour should commence within twenty-four hours. If the bitch fails to go into labour, this should alert you to the possibility of uterine inertia, and a Caesarian may be needed.

GIVING BIRTH

It is impossible in a book of this size to explain all the details of the actual whelping, but if you are a novice breeder, it is essential *to arrange for an experienced breeder to be present.*

The puppy should arrive, head-first, in a transparent sac. Most bitches will automatically know what to do, but a maiden bitch having her first litter, may be bewildered by what is happening. Speed is essential, and you must break the bag and clear the puppy's mouth by holding its head down and rubbing it with a towel until it breathes.

Hopefully, when the bitch hears the puppy squeak she will take over, sever the cord and eat the afterbirth. If, however, she is still not interested, you will have to sever the cord yourself. This should be done by massaging the blood in the cord between your finger and thumb, backwards and towards the puppy, and then cut the cord in front of your fingers, about two inches from the puppy's body. Apply a mild solution of iodine to congeal the blood, and place the puppy on one of the bitch's teats, and, with luck, she will start licking it, as it begins to feed.

During the period the bitch is having her puppies (nearly always in the night), give her an occasional drink of cold milk and honey, with a dash of brandy, to keep up her strength. I always try to take the bitch out, *on the lead,* to relieve herself. If you do not have her on the lead, she will make a mad dash back to her puppies before doing the necessary. One word of warning, when she squats to urinate, make sure a puppy doesn't 'pop out' at the same time. It once happened to me in the night, and luckily I was shining my torch on her and was able to catch the puppy as it appeared. It is always difficult to know when a bitch has finished whelping, and halfway through the delivery you will probably have a false alarm when she may stretch out and go to sleep. When you are pretty sure all the puppies have arrived, give the bitch a clean bed, a drink of warm milk with honey or glucose, and let her have a well-earned sleep, with all her family happily feeding.

POST-WHELPING

Within twelve hours of the bitch finishing whelping, I always arrange for the vet to call (never take the bitch to the vet, in these circumstances) to give her an antibiotic, and probably an injection of Oxytocin to remove any after-birth which may have been left in the bitch. The vet will also carefully examine the puppies to ascertain that they are all in good health. For a few days after whelping, the bitch will have a dirty brown or green vaginal discharge. This should cease in a few days, and then the bitch can be washed around her hindquarters and returned, completely dry, to her offspring.

CARE OF BITCH AND PUPPIES

The first three days of a puppy's life are vital, and I try to be in the room at all times (including sleeping) to make sure that the bitch has utmost peace and quiet (no visitors), and that no puppy is being pushed out by its brothers and sisters, or inadvertently squashed by the dam. For the first three weeks your time is mainly

The litter pictured just after whelping.

Puppies are great time-wasters, you can spend hours just watching them play together.

It is important to check that all the puppies are feeding from their mother.

As the puppies get bigger, the mother will spend less time with them, although some bitches are more maternal than others.

spent attending to the bitch, and her every whim, and for the following five weeks (after weaning) the puppies will be your main concern.

Your bitch will not want to leave her puppies, but every four hours she must be taken out to relieve herself. You will have to put her on a lead, and close the door behind you, or else she will be back in a flash. On one of these occasions, I arrange for someone to clean the whelping box, putting the puppies in the cardboard box while this is taking place. By the time the bitch returns, the puppies are back under the lamp on a lovely clean piece of bedding. After a few days, the bitch will not want to be in the box all the time; she will lie outside until she considers her offspring are in need of feeding.

THE BITCH'S DIET
One thing a novice breeder fails to appreciate is that the mother requires large amounts of food, and plenty of liquid, until the process of weaning begins. In the first few days after giving birth the bitch's motions will be very loose, and for the first twenty-four hours, a white diet (chicken, fish, rabbit) plus a very small amount of soaked biscuits, is strongly recommended.

With regard to the liquid intake, it is worth remembering that it is not necessary to give milk to produce milk; this can add to the diarrhoea problem. It is liquid that produces milk in the bitch, and with this in mind, I always leave large quantities of water available. It is advisable to put the bitch back on to a normal diet as soon as possible, and by the time eight puppies are two weeks old, the bitch will be needing approximately 3lb of meat and 1lb of soaked biscuits, with all her vitamins (especially calcium) added, plus one pint of diluted milk. The food is divided as follows:
7am: 1 pint diluted milk with honey or glucose, plus baby cereal.
10.30am: 4oz soaked biscuits, plus 12oz meat.
2pm: Repeat 10.30am meal.
6pm: Repeat 10.30am meal.
l0pm: Repeat 10.30am meal.
Remember to gradually decrease the bitch's rations as weaning begins.

NAIL TRIMMING
So far, the mother has attended to all her puppies' needs, but when they reach the age of five days, their claws will have become needle sharp and will require cutting. This is done by just taking off the points, being careful not to cut too far back. It is advisable to repeat this procedure once a week until the puppies are able to wear them down by running on a hard surface, otherwise they will scratch the bitch's stomach, causing her much discomfort.

WORMING
Your next duty with regard to the puppies will be to worm them. This should be done for the first time at about two to two-and-a-half weeks, so that the puppies' food can be used for its proper purpose, namely growth. For this first worming,use a treatment recommended by your vet and follow instructions as to frequency of treatment and dosage. In order to give the correct dosage, the puppies will need to be weighed accurately.

I worm the puppies in the evening and then get up early next morning to try and save the dam the awful job of having to eat the puppies' motions, which more than likely will be full of worms. Inevitably she will clean up some of the worms, and so will need worming herself. Each time I worm the puppies, I worm the bitch one week later until she has stopped coming in contact with them.

WEANING

This can be started at about two-and-a-half weeks, but I often leave it until three weeks, working on the basis that 'Mother's food is best'. The first thing I do is teach them to lap, using a simulated bitch's milk. Each puppy must be taught individually, and usually no problems are encountered. However, if one is slow to get the message, gently push its chin and lips into the milk, and soon all will be well.

In a few days I repeat the procedure with best quality raw chopped beef, putting a small amount on my finger and letting the puppy lick it off. Within a few days the puppies are having a saucer of milk three times a day each and 1oz of meat once a day. These amounts are gradually increased, and at this stage I change from powdered milk to an all-in milk feed. At approximately four weeks I add to the meat a small amount of soaked biscuits (puppy grade), and the revised diet should read:

7.30am: 1/4 pint milk feed.
l0am: 2oz meat, 1/2oz soaked biscuit, plus additives.
2pm: Repeat milk feed.
6pm: Repeat milk feed.
l0pm: Repeat meat feed, without additives.

At around this time, the puppies are moved to the outside kennel, and a small dish of water is put at their disposal. By this time the puppies are five weeks old, the mother will be seeing them less and less, and probably will not be sleeping with them at all. At this stage a puppy should weigh around 7lbs, and will now begin to eat you out of house and home. At six weeks old each puppy should be receiving the following diet:

8.30am: 1/2 pint milk feed.
lpm: $3_{1/2}$oz meat, plus 1oz soaked biscuit meal, plus additives.
5pm: Repeat breakfast.
9pm: Repeat lunch, without additives.
llpm: A few goodnight biscuits.

These amounts should be gradually increased, so that at eight weeks you should have reached the amounts shown on the diet sheet you received when collecting your puppy.

SELLING THE PUPPIES

The difficult moment of parting with your puppies is now at hand, and it is hoped that you will be as meticulous in your choice of owner, as your breeder was with you. Do not forget to give your new owners a folder, containing the necessary documents. Finally, be sure to offer an after sales service, keeping in touch with your host of new friends.

Chapter Eight

HEALTH CARE

Goldens are a hardy breed, and with common sense and attention to detail, visits to the vet can be reduced or kept to a minimum. Working on the basis that 'prevention is better than cure', the following tips are essential for the well-being of your Golden Retriever.

GENERAL MAINTENANCE

INOCULATIONS: Your puppy will have had its initial inoculations in the first few months of its life (See Chapter 2), but every twelve months for the rest of the dog's life, a booster is required, and these must *never* be missed.

EXERCISE: A fat dog is not a happy one, nor for that matter is a dog that is too thin. A Golden requires free-running exercise every day; it is no use restricting your dog all week and then going on a marathon at the weekend. Sensible exercise, combined with a correct balanced diet, should guarantee ideal body weight.

GROOMING: My dogs are groomed every day, but once or twice a week should suffice for the pet owner. Take the opportunity to inspect for anything that may be amiss such as running eyes, wax in the ears, growths, skin problems or cut pads.

WORMING: This has been covered in relation to puppies (see Chapter 2), but a strict worming regime is a must throughout a dog's life.

ECTOPARASITES: Ectoparasites include fleas, lice, ticks and mange. They live in or on the skin of your dog, and just as a child with the best home conditions can get 'hair nits,' so your dog can acquire these parasites.

FLEAS: These cause itching, and so your dog will soon be scratching. In bad cases, you can see thin elongated, brown wingless insects with long legs, running over the skin, and then jump off the animal. They are often in evidence in long dry summers, and attach to the dog on its head and face, around the neck and at the base of the tail. Flea droppings, which are often left in the dog, are black, hard and the size of grains of sand. Fleas live most of their cycle off the dog, and so it is essential not only to treat the dog with some form of insecticide, but also the dog's bedding and the edges of the house carpets as well.

LICE : These feed on the skin and lay eggs on the hair, and they are prevalent around the dog's neck and ears, and the inside of the thighs. They are light brown, fat and wingless, and must be treated with a prescribed insecticide. The treatment must be repeated in fourteen days in order to kill the newly-hatched lice.

TICKS: These brownish-white rounded insects, the size of a pea or bean, are usually caught when the dog goes through grass or shrubs where sheep have been. Ticks are suckling parasites, and they feed by sucking blood from the dog. They are most

Golden Retrievers are a hardy breed which need regular exercise, and there are few that can resist a dip in the water.

usually found on the head, neck and shoulders during the summer months. A tick attaches itself to the dog by its mouthpiece, and care must be taken that you do not leave the tick's head still embedded when you try to remove it, as this can cause severe skin infection. These parasites can be removed by using cotton-wool (cotton), well dampened with surgical spirit. If this is held in position, covering the tick, for approximately five minutes, the tick will loosen its hold.

MANGE: There are two common types: Sarcoptic or Follicular. Mange causes intense irritation which can result in the dog scratching until blood appears on the affected area. The affected areas are generally around the head, the neck, the ears, under body, and the inside of the thighs and forelegs. Sarcoptic Mange is readily transmissible from dog to dog, so it is essential that all dogs living in the same area are treated. Your vet will advise on the most suitable brand of insecticidal shampoo to use. With all skin complaints, including Eczema, the quicker you start veterinary treatment, the better. It is, however, of great importance that you provide your vet with as much information as possible. This includes such matters as the type of fluids used to clean the kitchen floor and carpets, and the brand of aerosol sprays that are used in the house. This may seem irrelevant, but your dog may be allergic to one of these products, and the treatment prescribed by your vet could be seriously undermined.

GENERAL OBSERVATIONS

MOTIONS: A dog's motions are a good indicator of its general state of health. If you detect any looseness, it is a sign of a possible problem. Quite often the trouble is caused by diet, and this can easily be adjusted by feeding rice and white meat, or fish, plus some medicine to settle the stomach. Your vet will advise the most suitable brand to use. If the condition persists and turns to diarrhoea, the problem may be an infection of some description, and you should seek further advice from your vet.

SICKNESS AND VOMITING: The golden rule in this situation is that whenever a dog is sick, *never* administer anything by the mouth: no food, no liquid, no medicine. Starve your dog for twelve or twenty-four hours. You can let the dog lick ice cubes to prevent dehydration. If no further sickness has occurred then introduce a diet of white meat or fish plus boiled rice, the secret being 'a little often', i.e. divide his normal meal into four small ones. Small drinks can now be given but do not at this stage leave water freely available.

REFUSAL OF FOOD: If your dog is reluctant to eat, never try to force-feed. If the condition persists, it is a sign that all is not well, and you should contact your vet.

TEMPERATURE: One of my most valuable pieces of equipment is a clinical thermometer. At the first sign of any trouble I take the dog's temperature, which in normal circumstances should be 101.5 degrees Fahrenheit. I usually smear the end of the thermometer with Vaseline and then insert it into the rectum, gently pressing it sideways against the wall of the rectum. If the thermometer is inserted in a straight line, then, more than likely, it will merely be in the middle of a motion not yet excreted, and a correct reading will be almost impossible. Always be careful to keep hold of the thermometer once inserted into the rectum, as the muscles of the dog's rectum can suck in the thermometer. I cannot stress too strongly that a rise in temperature above 102.5 degrees F., coupled with any of the above mentioned symptoms or conditions, is a clear indication that veterinary assistance is needed *immediately*.

COMMON AILMENTS

Like humans, all dogs are prone to certain ailments, although a fit dog that is fed a well-balanced diet is less likely to be troubled by such complaints. Ideally, your Golden Retriever would only visit the vet once a year for its booster inoculation. In reality, your dog is more likely to be affected by one of the more common canine ailments, and prompt treatment will ensure a swift recovery.

ANAL GLANDS: If you see your dog 'dragging its bottom' along the floor, or notice a strange smell from its rear end, then probably the anal glands require attention. These glands are situated at either side of the rectum, and occasionally they need emptying. The vet will perform this simple operation, by squeezing the glands out. Sometimes they empty themselves when the dog is over-excited or nervous, hence the smell.

PYOMETRA: This is more likely to occur in older or middle-aged bitches. It flares up in the period of oestrus cycle known as metoestrus, one or two months after the bitch has been in season. It is caused by fluid gathering in the uterus. The signs to look for include: Excessive drinking, increased urination, raised temperature, no appetite, sickness, and often distension of the stomach. Immediate veterinary attention is critical, and a hysterectomy operation will probably be needed.

KENNEL COUGH: Your dog can be inoculated against this very contagious disease, which can be extremely dangerous in young puppies. Coughing usually develops five to ten days after contact with an infected animal. A natural 'breeding ground' for this disease is at shows or in boarding kennels, where a number of dogs are gathered together. Although the dog may appear lively and well, prompt treatment by your vet is essential and, unfortunately, isolation is a necessity.

CYSTITIS: This is caused by inflammation of the bladder. Symptoms include constant passing of urine, or attempts to do so. If a bitch is affected, there may be evidence of obvious discomfort when she rises from the squatting position.

Cystitis is often the result of an infection, but can be caused by grit, stones, or a growth in the bladder. Veterinary assistance is a must, and you will need to take a urine sample with you, in a bottle. How do I get the urine in the bottle? I hear you ask. When the dog or bitch has started to urinate, place a dish under the required spot, and then fill the bottle from the dish. Easy when you know how!

GROWTHS: Retrievers, in general, are somewhat prone to growths or tumours. These are more likely to occur in old age, but they can occur in young stock as well. They can range from skin growths to internal tumours, and they can either be benign or malignant. If in doubt, seek veterinary advice immediately.

FALSE OR PHANTOM PREGNANCY: This condition can occur when a bitch has been in season, and it will come to light about nine weeks following the season; the time she would have had her puppies – if she had been mated. Symptoms include: listlessness, increased thirst, and perhaps, loss of appetite. Milk often appears in the mammary glands and the bitch begins to make her bed for the arrival of the non-existent puppies. The treatment for this condition includes feeding fish or white meat, instead of red meat, and to cut down on liquids. Instead of leaving water constantly available, I usually give the bitch small drinks at specific times. If the condition does not appear to be responding, or is prolonged (it can last up to seven weeks if not checked) then contact your veterinary surgeon for advice.

HEREDITARY CONDITIONS

The Golden Retriever is a hardy, no-nonsense breed, built on working lines, but there are some problems which can arise, and all owners should be aware of them.

HIP DYSPLASIA: Most breeds suffer from hip dysplasia to some extent. Even if you bought from a specialised breeder (See Chapter 2), there is no guarantee that your puppy will be free from this condition, although the odds of getting satisfactory hips will have been increased by the care that the breeder has taken in this respect.

Hip dysplasia is an abnormal development of the hip joint, and there are specially set up schemes to evaluate the problem. The dogs hips are X-rayed after the age of twelve months, each hip being scored from 0 - 53; the lower the score, the better. The average score for Golden Retrievers is approximately 19 in total.

The symptoms of hip dysplasia appear in a puppy from about six months of age. An affected puppy may suffer difficulty or discomfort when getting up from a sitting or lying position; the rear legs may be prone to stiffness or lameness, and when the dog is walking, you may observe a swaying action from side to side of the rear end. The above symptoms can most certainly be exacerbated by the over-exercising and over-feeding of a young puppy.

The decision as to whether you decide to have your puppy X-rayed and hip-scored when it is twelve months old, is entirely yours. However, if you intend breeding from your dog or bitch, then you would be strongly advised to do so.

HEREDITARY CATARACT AND PROGRESSIVE RETINAL ATROPHY: Both are conditions of the eye, and affect vision. Hereditary Cataract affects some Goldens

The Golden Retriever is a no-nonsense breed, built on working lines.

but Progressive Retinal Atrophy is less common. Your breeders' stock will have had to be free from both these conditions, to be allowed to breed. If you decide to breed, you will have to have your dog's eyes tested under one of the special schemes.

ENTROPION: This is not as common in Goldens today as used to be the case. It occurs when the eyelids turn in, causing the eyelashes to rub on the cornea, and this causes the dog great distress. The condition can be recognised from an early age, and surgery is required to correct it.

OSTEOCHONDRITIS: This affects large sized, fast-growing breeds, including Goldens. It can affect any of the joint, although the elbow joint seems to be most commonly affected in Goldens. Intermittent lameness is first noticed when the puppy is about four months of age, and veterinary advice is essential. Surgery can prove successful. There is some debate as to the cause of this condition; it may be hereditary, but it has also been attributed to excessive supplementation of the diet, over exercise, or traumatic episodes.

EPILEPSY: This is not always an hereditary condition. It is most often seen as a fit or convulsive seizure, which usually occurs when a dog is resting or sleeping. Symptoms include: paddling movements, shaking of the muscles with spasms, and sometimes involuntary passing of urine. If this occurs – do not panic. This is not an emergency, and nothing will be achieved by rushing straight to the vet, or trying to get the vet to come out to you. Give your dog, and yourself, time to calm down, and then go to see the vet and give a detailed description of your dog's condition, so that the appropriate treatment can be prescribed.